The Principal's Guide to Attention Deficit Hyperactivity Disorder

Elaine K. McEwan

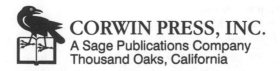

CORWIN PRESS, INC.
A Sage Publications Company
Thousand Oaks, California

For information:

Corwin Press, Inc.
A Sage Publications Company
2455 Teller Road
Thousand Oaks, California 91320
E-mail: order@corwin.sagepub.com

SAGE Publications Ltd.
6 Bonhill Street
London EC2A 4PU
United Kingdom

SAGE Publications India Pvt. Ltd.
M-32 Market
Greater Kailash I
New Delhi 110 048 India

Printed in the United States of America

McEwan, Elaine K., 1941-
   The principal's guide to attention deficit hyperactivity disorder/
   by Elaine K. McEwan.
      p. cm.
   Includes index.
   ISBN 0-8039-6532-X (pbk.: acid-free paper). — ISBN 0-8039-6531-1
   (cloth: acid-free paper)
   1. Attention-deficit-disordered children—Education—United
States. 2. Attention-deficit hyperactivity disorder—United States.
3. School principals—United States. I. Title.
   LC4713.4.M39 1997
   371.93—dc21   97-4905

98 99 00 01 02 03 04 10 9 8 7 6 5 4 3 2 1

Editorial Assistant: Kristen L. Gibson
Production Editor: Michele Lingre
Production Assistant: Karen Wiley
Typesetter/Designer: Danielle Dillahunt
Cover Designer: Marcia M. Rosenburg
Print Buyer: Anna Chin

CONTENTS

ABOUT THE AUTHOR

Elaine K. McEwan is a private educational consultant with the McEwan-Adkins Group offering training for school districts in leadership and team building, writing workshops for children, and parenting seminars. A former teacher, librarian, principal, and assistant superintendent for instruction in a suburban Chicago school district, she is the author of more than two dozen books, including titles for parents and teachers (*Attention Deficit Disorder*), fiction for middle-grade students (*Joshua McIntire Series*), and guides for administrators (*Leading Your Team to Excellence*). She is the education columnist for the *Oro Valley Explorer* newspaper in Arizona, a contributing editor to several parenting magazines on educational issues, and can be heard on a variety of syndicated radio and television programs helping parents solve schooling problems.

She was honored by the Illinois Principals Association as an outstanding instructional leader, by the Illinois State Board of Education with an Award of Excellence in the Those Who Excel Program, and by the National Association of Elementary School Principals as the National Distinguished Principal from Illinois for 1991.

McEwan received her undergraduate degree in education from Wheaton College and graduate degrees in library science and educational administration from Northern Illinois University.

She lives with her husband and business partner, E. Raymond Adkins, in Oro Valley, Arizona.

INTRODUCTION

When I began my teaching career in the early 1960s, we had not yet begun to assign the ADD (attention deficit disorder) label to children. Children with symptoms of impulsivity and problems with concentration were thought to be brain injured, minimally brain damaged, hyperactive, or hyperkinetic. I was actually one of those children myself, and I had a great deal of empathy for my students who were similarly blessed. I drove the teacher in my one-room schoolhouse classroom to distraction with my constant interruptions and hyperactivity. But she always managed to couch her report card comments positively: "Elaine needs a hobby to keep her occupied." "Elaine's energy needs to be channeled into positive interests." She stopped short of asking me to quit bugging her. I was always finished first, so she put me to work helping others. This was my first experience with cooperative learning in action. When I moved into the upper elementary grades, my energies were used in administrative tasks—answering the telephone, running the mimeograph machine, grading papers, and straightening out storage closets. These were excellent preparations for my later administrative career.

I talked and moved nonstop—often running wildly in circles in the kitchen, pretending to be a horse, until the day I ran smack into a corner and collapsed on the floor sobbing as blood gushed out of my head. My mother was always in tears over the things I ruined—her new refrigerator scarred by my ice skates, her glass hurricane lamps shattered by a falling table, my aunt's antique clock smashed to bits. I left a wake of havoc and ruin.

Somehow, I learned to survive in school. I'm sure the multigraded, open classroom helped. And my after-school jobs were a good outlet for my excess energy. I started working for my father in his grocery store when I was 6 years old. I stocked shelves, put potatoes in 10-pound bags, and swept the front porch. When he bought a department store, I began to work there at the age of 12—marking merchandise, decorating windows, and waiting on customers. My confidence grew as I learned to sell overalls to farmers and fit babies for their first pairs of shoes.

In school, I learned to sit in the front of the room, keep my mouth shut, and keep my hands busy taking copious notes. Classmates teased me for recording everything the teacher said—even the jokes. I started studying and organizing for exams weeks in advance. I knew my weaknesses well and learned to compensate for them. Fortunately, I had a lot of love and reinforcement along the way. I believed that I could do or be anything I wanted to be. My home was organized and structured. Today, I might be diagnosed with ADHD (attention deficit hyperactivity disorder). But in the late 1940s, I was simply a child with a lot of energy that needed to be focused. I learned from personal experience what children with ADHD need.

As a fifth-grade teacher in the 1960s, I provided structure, organization, expectations, good home-school communication, and lots of hands-on learning for all of my students, many of them with ADHD. When one approach didn't work, we tried another. There was no child who couldn't behave and learn in my classroom. As an elementary school principal in the 1980s, I continued to believe that all children could learn and succeed in school. And that is the philosophy I espouse in this book. Children with ADHD can succeed at home, in school, and in the community. They can manage their difficulties. They will grow up to be successful adults who can make a positive contribution to our society. Our obligation as educators is to accept, love, and understand them and then find ways to help them succeed.

Every author approaches the task of writing with certain assumptions and biases about the subject. Here are mine:

- Children with ADHD have the potential to be creative, useful, productive, and successful members of society.

- There is no stereotypical child with ADHD. Each child is unique, and each combination of symptoms will vary.

- ADHD is a biologically based condition that has lifelong implications.
- Children with ADHD are at risk of failure in school, social rejection, and behavioral complication unless educators and parents work together as a team.

Furthermore, every author has certain goals and purposes in mind for the reader. Here's what I hope you will gain from reading this book:

- An understanding of what ADHD is, its causes, and possible treatment options
- A working knowledge of the legalities of designing a program to meet the educational needs of children with ADHD
- A repertoire of ideas, strategies, and services that you can use in your school to maximize learning for students with ADHD
- Positive and productive ways to work with parents and students to build a strong home-school connection.

The Principal's Guide to Attention Deficit Hyperactivity Disorder[1] is designed to be a practical, hands-on book. Here's what you will encounter in the chapters ahead.

Chapter One provides an overview of ADHD, describing the range of symptoms and answering the most commonly asked questions about the disorder.

Chapter Two discusses the legalities of ADHD, describes the special education laws you need to know, and suggests a variety of options for providing services to students with ADHD.

Chapter Three shows you how to evaluate students for ADHD in your school setting and provides more than 20 helpful forms and checklists to guide the process.

Chapter Four points out possible treatment options, describes the most commonly prescribed medications, and evaluates many of the alternative types of treatment that are often intriguing to parents.

Chapter Five shows you how to work effectively with classroom teachers by providing instructional strategies, interventions, and accommodations for working with students who have ADHD. It also contains checklists and evaluative standards to help you determine which teachers work best with children with ADHD.

Chapter Six offers some suggestions for that most challenging of assignments—working with the parents of students with ADHD.

Last, there are several helpful appendices containing resource and reference material. For example, Resource A contains descriptions of the nearly two dozen families I interviewed as part of my background research into the school experiences of families living with ADHD. Resource B contains a complete listing of organizations and resources for both educators and parents.

Meeting the educational needs of children with ADHD is an adventure. There is much uncharted territory, so the maps may not always be accurate or even available. But in these words of advice taken from one of my favorite children's books,

> If tomorrow morning the sky falls, have clouds for breakfast.
> If the bus doesn't come—catch a fast cloud.
> If your horse needs shoes—let him use his wings.[2]

In other words—do not become so bound to what has been that you do not see the exciting possibilities for what can be.

NOTE

1. Selected sections of this book were previously published in *Attention Deficit Disorder* by Elaine K. McEwan. Reprinted by permission of the publisher Harold Shaw Publishers, Wheaton, IL. © 1995.

2. Cooper Edens, *If You're Afraid of the Dark,* (New York: Green Tiger Press, 1979).

To Linda Colson, Shirley Justin-Wolff,
Becky Rosenthal, and Lisa York
The Dream PPS Team

1

UNDERSTANDING ATTENTION DEFICIT HYPERACTIVITY DISORDER (ADHD)

Fidgety Phil

"Phil, stop acting like a worm,
The table is no place to squirm."
thus speaks the father to his son,
severely says it, not in fun.
Mother frowns and looks around
although she doesn't make a sound.
But, Philipp will not take advise,
he'll have his way at any price.
He turns,
and churns,
he wiggles
and jiggles
Here and there on the chair.
"Phil, these twists I cannot bear."

—Heinrich Hoffman,
1863 Nursery Rhyme

If you're slightly confused about what attention deficit hyperactivity disorder (ADHD) is and what the "politically correct" position is on its existence and treatment, you're not alone. Articles about ADHD in educational journals and even popular magazines invariably draw

1

dozens of competing Letters to the Editor from parents, educators, and health care professionals. The letters argue for and against labeling children, for and against providing special education services, and for and against medication as a treatment alternative. There's a lot of finger pointing at pediatricians for overprescribing, at schools for their failure to provide more receptive learning environments, and at parents for not being better disciplinarians. I write a weekly question-and-answer column on education in our local newspaper and receive multiple questions each year about the frustrations of helping a child with an attention disorder navigate the rough waters of schooling. Even Congress got into the ADHD debate in the early 1990s as the need for special education labels and services for students with ADHD was heatedly discussed during the reauthorization of the Individuals with Disabilities Act. The Department of Education subsequently issued a policy letter (see Resource C) that stated that students with the disorder can get special help under existing rules without changing the federal special education law to explicitly name attention deficit disorder as a handicapping condition. While the discussion-debate continues at policy levels and in the media, you, the building principal, must deal on a daily basis with frazzled and frustrated teachers, demanding and insistent parents, and kids whose energy levels and creativity for everything but schoolwork defy the imagination.

I hope the answers to the most commonly asked questions about ADHD that follow will give you the information you need to help your teachers, parents, and most important, your students with ADHD find success in school.

DOES ADHD REALLY EXIST?

There are some who would argue against the existence of attention deficit disorder (ADD) as a diagnostic category. After all, there is no laboratory test that can conclusively determine its existence, and the symptoms when described for the average lay person sound suspiciously like characteristics that most people have at one time or other in their lives. Who hasn't lost his or her checkbook and car keys, had a hard time concentrating in class, or impulsively said the wrong thing at a party. The arguments of author Thomas Armstrong, for example, can almost make one believe ADHD is part of a giant alien conspiracy. In his book, *The Myth of the A.D.D. Child*, he slam dunks just about everybody:

[The A.D.D. phenomenon] is a recent historical development that represents a confluence of parent advocacy groups, legislative efforts, psychological studies, pharmaceutical advances, and psychiatric endorsements. A.D.D. isn't an educational "virus" that's been lurking in the brains of our children for centuries waiting for a chance to spring into action. Instead, A.D.D. is a construct that was essentially invented in the cognitive psychology laboratories of our nation's (and Canada's) universities, and then given life by the American Psychiatric Association, the U.S. Department of Education, and the chemical laboratories of the world's pharmaceutical corporations."[1]

Author Thom Hartmann has also added his two cents to the ADD controversy by hypothesizing that individuals with ADD are just descendants of the hunters of ancient times who roamed the wilderness killing prey and warding off danger.[2] The restless, impulsive, and fast-moving attentional characteristics of these hunters have descended into today's children and adults with ADD. It's an interesting idea, but it doesn't have much to do with school on Monday morning.

As an educator, you probably don't have a lot of time to speculate about conspiracy theories or anthropological hypotheses. The learning difficulties and behavioral challenges presented by a substantial number of your students do indeed exist. And you have very real legal obligations and responsibilities as a school principal to meet the needs of these students. What you need is help and soon.

WHERE DID IT COME FROM?

Children with symptoms of impulsivity and problems with concentration were originally labeled as brain injured, minimally brain damaged, hyperactive, and hyperkinetic. More recent and research-based terms include attention deficit disorder, attention deficit disorder with hyperactivity, attention deficit hyperactivity disorder, and undifferentiated attention deficit disorder. Authors, physicians, educators, psychologists, and researchers often use the terms interchangeably. But the symptoms that characterize the attention deficit disorders as a group—hyperactivity, impulsivity, and inattention—remain constant. Regardless of the precise label, ADHD continues to baffle, intrigue, frustrate, and fascinate parents and professionals alike.

The validity of ADHD as a bonafide disorder has been subject to scrutiny, skepticism, and even downright hostility in the past two decades. A 1975 book by Schrag and Divoky, *The Myth of the Hyperactive Child and Other Means of Control*[3] painted a grim picture of children purported to have ADHD and the medications used to treat them. The Church of Scientology conducted a legal vendetta of sorts in the middle to late 1980s, suing school boards, physicians, the American Psychiatric Association, principals, and teachers to prevent the use of Ritalin™ as a medication to treat children with ADHD. Alfie Kohn, a respected education writer, questioned the existence of the disorder in a 1989 Atlantic Monthly article.[4] ADHD has been called "the yuppie disease of the '90s" and "a highly debatable and pseudomedical concept." But for parents of children with ADHD, the problem is very real.

Weary of hearing surreptitious and snide comments about ADHD being a "cop-out for parents and kids who can't follow the rules" or a "racket for the medical profession," parents have joyously greeted the recent news of scientific investigations that give conclusive supporting evidence that ADHD is not a figment of some frantic parent's imagination but a real disorder, the result of physiological differences in the neurochemistry of the brain. Children with ADHD are unable to inhibit or direct their behavior, through no fault of their own. They are not always capable of the personal management skills and "directedness" needed for school success. The early and pervasive onset of this disorder clearly suggests that poor parenting, poor instruction, learning disabilities, or any other sociological or psychological process—or any combination of these—are not the causes of ADHD.

ADHD was first described in the middle 1800s when children who were recovering from nervous-system diseases or injuries were observed to have ADHD-like symptoms. In the early 20th century, a lecturer to the Royal College of Physicians described a group of youngsters who were aggressive, defiant, and resistant to discipline while also having problems with attention to tasks. After an outbreak of encephalitis in the 1940s left children with symptoms similar to those of hyperactive children, it was hypothesized that hyperactive children were brain damaged. After further research determined that hyperactive children were not brain damaged, the label was changed to *minimal brain dysfunction*. It was not until 1965 that a diagnostic category was first established by the American Psychiatric Association, called *hyperkinetic reaction of childhood*. Hyperactivity was defined not as a biological problem but as an environmental one. This set the stage for several years of "mommy bashing" in which ADHD-like behaviors were blamed on environmental conditions and poor parenting.

However, recognition that ADHD was a legitimate neurological disorder was affirmed when the American Psychiatric Association first established the diagnosis, "attention deficit disorder with or without hyperactivity" (DSM-III) in 1980. Still in question, however, was the importance of hyperactivity as a symptom or defining criterion, often causing frustration and confusion for parents and educators. Initially, the symptom of hyperactivity was seen as a related characteristic, one that would create subtypes of the disorder based on its presence or absence. A child could have ADD whether he or she exhibited hyperactivity or not. However, when the DSM-III-R was published in 1987, the disorder was relabeled as "attention deficit-hyperactivity disorder, and the subtyping of "without hyperactivity" was eliminated. Researchers were still unclear as to whether the "without hyperactivity" category was a subtype of attention deficit-hyperactivity disorder (ADHD) or a different category altogether. So, a category of "undifferentiated attention-deficit disorder" was created for children that displayed marked inattention but did not have signs of impulsiveness and hyperactivity. The new edition of the *Diagnostic and Statistical Manual of Mental Disorders* (DSM-IV) now describes three types of the disorder:

Attention-Deficit/Hyperactivity Disorder

A. Either (1) or (2):

(1) six (or more) of the following symptoms of inattention have persisted for at least six months to a degree that is maladaptive and inconsistent with developmental level:

Inattention

(a) often fails to give close attention to details or makes careless mistakes in schoolwork, work, or other activities

(b) often has difficulty sustaining attention in tasks or play activities

(c) often does not seem to listen when spoken to directly

(d) often does not follow through on instructions and fails to finish schoolwork, chores, or duties in the workplace (not due to oppositional behavior or failure to understand instructions)

(e) often has difficulties organizing tasks and activities

NOTE: Reprinted with permission. American Psychiatric Association: Diagnostic and Statistical Manual of Mental Disorders, 4th Ed. Washington DC, American Psychiatric Association, 1994.

    (f) often avoids, dislikes, or is reluctant to engage in tasks that require sustained mental effort (such as schoolwork or homework)

    (g) often loses things necessary for tasks or activities (e.g., toys, school assignments, pencils, books, or tools)

    (h) is often easily distracted by extraneous stimuli

    (i) is often forgetful in daily activities

(2) six (or more) of the following symptoms of *hyperactivity-impulsivity* have persisted for at least six months to a degree that is maladaptive and inconsistent with developmental level:

Hyperactivity

    (a) often fidgets with hands or feet or squirms in seat

    (b) often leaves seat in classroom or in other situations in which remaining seated is expected

    (c) often runs about or climbs excessively in situations where it is inappropriate (in adolescents or adults, may be limited to subjective feelings of restlessness)

    (d) often has difficulty playing or engaging in leisure activities quietly

    (e) is often "on the go" or often acts as if "driven by a motor"

    (f) often talks excessively

Impulsivity

    (g) often blurts out answers before questions have been completed

    (h) often has difficulty awaiting turn

    (i) often interrupts or intrudes on others (e.g., butts into conversations or games)

B.   Some hyperactive-impulsive or inattentive symptoms that caused impairment were present before age 7 years.

C.   Some impairment from the symptoms is present in two or more settings (e.g., at school [or work] and at home).

D.   There must be clear evidence of clinically significant impairment in social, academic, or occupational functioning.

E.   The symptoms do not occur exclusively during the course of a Pervasive Developmental Disorder, Schizophrenia, or other Psychotic Disorder, and are not better accounted for by another mental disorder (e.g., Mood Disorder, Anxiety Disorder, Dissociative Disorder, or a Personality Disorder).

314.01 Attention-Deficit/Hyperactivity Disorder, Combined Type: if both criteria A (1) and A (2) are met for the past six months.

314.00 Attention-Deficit/Hyperactivity Disorder, Predominantly Inattentive Type: if criterion A (1) is met but not criterion A (2) for past six months

314.01 Attention-Deficit/Hyperactivity Disorder, Predominantly Hyperactive-Impulsive Type: if criterion A(2) is met but not criterion A (1) for the past six months[5]

For purposes of clarity and brevity in this book, we will use the acronym ADHD to include all three ADDs.

ADHD is a medical syndrome rather than a disease. A syndrome is more difficult for professionals to diagnose because it must be determined whether a given collection of symptoms exhibited by an individual genuinely characterize the syndrome, are merely developmental delays that will disappear over time, or are symptoms of some other problem completely. The developmental nature of ADHD means that a child does not acutely acquire it nor does he or she really ever outgrow it.

Diagnosing ADHD is difficult because almost all of the symptoms included in the syndrome will be exhibited by most children at one time or another in their developmental history. What child hasn't forgotten to take out the garbage without several reminders, interrupted constantly at the dinner table, or forgotten a homework assignment? The critical difference between a child with ADHD and a child who is "immature" or is "misbehaving" is the number, severity, and constancy of the symptoms. Therefore, having an agreed-on list of symptoms, a time frame during which those symptoms must be present, and a degree to which they must affect a child's functioning in social, academic, and family settings are especially important for diagnostic purposes.

The disciplines that diagnose, treat, and prescribe for children with ADHD (medicine, psychology, psychiatry, and education) are constantly expanding and changing as further research and discoveries are made about what ADHD is, what its causes might be, and how best to help children and adults who have this disorder.

IS ADHD COMMON?

ADHD is the most common reason a child is referred to a psychologist or psychiatrist. Although figures vary slightly depending on the research study, the consensus is that ADHD occurs in 3% to 5% of the

8

population. About 1 child in 20 will have ADHD. Although the ratio of males to females diagnosed with ADHD is about 6 to 1, females are probably underidentified. Researchers suspect that the ratio is closer to 3 to 1 in actuality. Girls are more likely to be identified with the type of ADHD that does not exhibit symptoms of hyperactivity and impulsivity. Unfortunately, they may be labeled simply "daydreamers," "spacey," or "social butterflies," and their problems will go undetected and untreated. Studies show that ADHD occurs almost as frequently in Europe, Africa, Australia, and South America as it does in the United States. More cases may be diagnosed in the United States, however, because of the quality and quantity of research being conducted in this area.

WHAT CAUSES ADHD?

The causes of ADHD have been the subject of much scrutiny and study. The most current scientific consensus is that ADHD is primarily an inherited condition. Although brain injury can cause symptoms of inattention, hyperactivity, and impulsivity, less then 5% of children with ADHD, whose records have been examined, give evidence of brain injury. Whereas environmental influences, such as poor parental practices or family stress, may increase the severity of the disorder or interfere with a successful treatment plan, they do not *cause* ADHD.

To the beleaguered parents who were castigated by critics for their poor parenting, to children who were labeled undisciplined and lazy, and to physicians who were accused of padding their case loads to finance trips to the continent, a landmark study by Alan Zametkin and his colleagues at the National Institute of Mental Health in 1990 provided the collective opportunity to say "I told you so."

Using a scanning technique called *positron emission tomography*, which allows study of the brain's use of glucose, the researchers described a significant difference between usage in individuals with a history of ADHD and those without such a history.[6] Adults with ADHD use glucose, the brain's main energy source, at a lesser rate than do adults without ADHD. This reduced brain metabolism rate was most evident in the portion of the brain that is important for attention, handwriting, motor control, and inhibition of responses. This study along with others has convinced researchers that ADHD is a neurological disorder.

More recently, researchers at the National Institute of Mental Health reported finding further evidence that ADHD has a neurobiological basis. The study examined 112 boys, aged 5 to 18 years, half of whom had been diagnosed with ADHD and half who did not have the disorder. Researchers found statistically significant size differences in certain regions of the boys' brains regions that control functions such as inhibition and planning. They also found that the boys with ADHD had symmetrical right and left sides of their brains; for the control group, the right side of the brain was larger than the left.[7] Further research is necessary to determine the effects of medication on brain size (because some of the boys had previously been treated with stimulant medication) as well as testing with girls to determine if the findings hold true across gender lines.

WHAT DOESN'T CAUSE ADHD?

Poor parenting has taken a lot of the blame for the behaviors exhibited by kids with ADHD. Nobody knows this better than Mary Ellen Corcoran. Mary Ellen has been a classroom teacher, Title I Coordinator, and is currently an inclusion facilitator. She is no stranger to the ins and outs of the special education maze. But as a parent, she sees many issues from the "other side." Her adolescent son has ADHD. She speaks for all parents of children with ADHD very eloquently:

> I wish I had gotten some early advice on how to deal with criticism, both overt and perceived. Parents need to feel responsible for getting the proper help and for implementing appropriate behavioral measures. However, taking too personally the comments by family, friends, and strangers at the grocery store is counterproductive. It often feels like you can't win, because even when positive programming works, and the child behaves, you get snide comments about bribery. "Why can't your child just be good?" they say. Maintaining a positive view of oneself as a parent is helpful in what is perhaps the central task of parenting an ADHD child: building self-esteem in a kid who gets into lots of trouble.

Although unstructured homes and lack of discipline can certainly exacerbate the symptoms of ADHD, they don't cause them. Food coloring, additives, preservatives, and salicylates don't cause ADHD either. In 1973, Dr. Benjamin Feingold hypothesized that these omni-present ingredients of junk food were the cause of hyperactivity. The theory drew a lot of popular press and struck a common-sense chord in parents. Most of us were looking for a good reason to ban junk food. Although Feingold reported that the additive-free diet reduced ADHD symptoms, many carefully controlled studies by independent re-searchers have failed to replicate his findings. This is not to say that a healthy diet is not beneficial for a child and that some children with ADHD may have problems with allergies that are related to food additives. But researchers looking for a causal link between ADHD and diet did not find one. "At this point, continuing claims that dietary substances are a major contributor to ADHD cannot be taken seriously, and the burden of proof that they do must rest with those who would propose such etiologies."[8]

Other unproven causes of ADHD include the following:

Sugar

In the mid-1980s, refined sugar became the suspected culprit of ADHD symptoms. Studies at the National Institute of Mental Health, the University of Iowa, and the University of Kentucky were never able to demonstrate that sugar produced significant effects on chil-dren's behavior or learning. "The current scientific consensus is that sugar does not produce large or clinically important effects on chil-dren's behavior and learning and certainly does not produce the clinical syndrome of ADHD."[9]

Elevated Lead Levels

Although there is evidence to show that body lead levels are associated to a very small degree with hyperactivity and inattention in the general population of children, body lead is unlikely to be a major cause of ADHD in children.[10]

Smoking or Alcohol Consumption During Pregnancy

Although cigarette smoking and alcohol consumption during preg-nancy are heavier in mothers of children having ADHD, the research shows no clear direction of causality between smoking and alcohol consumption during pregnancy and the incidence of ADHD.

Lighting

In the mid-1970s, cool-white fluorescent lighting was hypothesized to cause ADHD with the soft x-rays and radio frequencies that are emitted. No relationship was found.

WHAT ELSE MAY CAUSE ADHD-LIKE SYMPTOMS?

The diagnosis of ADHD is not always easy to make. There are numerous emotional and physiological conditions that mimic ADHD and serve to confuse parents, educators, and professionals. Beware of rushing to judgment regarding a student in your school. A comprehensive examination and evaluation by a psychiatrist (for emotional and mental disorders) or a physician (for the possible medical conditions) should be part of any diagnostic workup for ADHD.

Emotional Disorders that Look Like ADHD

Oppositional Defiant Disorder and Conduct Disorder

Children with these disorders are defiant and difficult to handle. They don't follow rules or do what they are told. But unlike the child with ADHD who may also exhibit these symptoms because he or she attempts to comply and can't, the oppositional child simply refuses. Defiance in a child with these disorders is often directed toward the mother initially. His or her behavior may lack the impulsive, disinhibited nature of the child with ADHD. These disorders are more likely to be associated with poor parenting skills or a dysfunctional family system, whereas ADHD is not the result of either.

Anxiety or Mood Disorders

Anxiety disorders cause fretful and worrisome behaviors in children. Their restlessness is not the "driven" or hyperactive variety that is seen in children with ADHD. Children with anxiety disorders are not usually disruptive but are more likely to be socially withdrawn. Children with anxiety and mood disorders do not have the preschool history of hyperactivity and impulsive behavior associated with the child with ADHD. When treated with stimulant medication that is prescribed for children with ADHD, these children often become teary and agitated.

Thought Disorders

Children with thought disorders demonstrate unusual thinking patterns. They may fixate on strange ideas or objects and frequently have motor mannerisms that are peculiar. Children with ADHD do not typically present the odd fascinations and strange aversions seen in children with thought disorders.

Depression and Anxiety

A depressed child may confuse the observer with a variety of behaviors, some that mimic ADHD without hyperactivity (e.g., sad, lethargic, unmotivated) or symptoms that are similar to ADHD with hyperactivity (e.g., acting out, inattentiveness).

Bipolar Disorder

This disorder is a manic-depressive illness and is diagnosed much less frequently than depression or ADHD. Many children with bipolar disorder show periods of hyperactivity and are also likely to be aggressive and antisocial. Stimulant medication administered to children with bipolar disorder may result in a psychotic or manic episode. Lithium™ is usually prescribed for this disorder.

Medical Conditions That May Be Confused With ADHD

Hypothyroidism and Hyperthyroidism

The rapid heartbeat, irritability, and overactivity that are symptoms of hypothyroidism and hyperthyroidism can be confused with ADHD. These symptoms will be intensified if treated with stimulant medication.

Side Effects of Medications

Some medications given to children for other medical problems may produce symptoms that mimic ADHD. Two antiseizure medications for epilepsy, phenobarbital and Dilantin™, can produce symptoms of hyperactivity and irritability. A popular asthma medication, theophylline (sold under the popular names of Theo-dur™ and Slo-bid™) can also cause ADHD-like symptoms.

Rare Genetic Disorders and
Gross Neurological Impairment

There are several rare genetic disorders that have ADHD symptoms as an associated problem. They include neurofibromatosis, Tourette syndrome, and fragile X syndrome. Children with these disorders, however, will have many associated physical problems as well as learning difficulties. Other impairments that may result in problems with attention, impulsivity, and hyperactivity are pituitary gland dysfunctions, fetal alcohol syndrome, Williams syndrome, injury to fetus from infection or trauma, hypoxia, and premature birth.

Narcolepsy

This sleep disorder, which results in frequent uncontrolled episodes of falling asleep, can produce symptoms of impaired attention, memory loss, and fluctuating levels of alertness.

Sleep Apnea

Children who exhibit symptoms of hyperactivity, inattentiveness, forgetfulness, irritability, or who conversely are underactive, sluggish, and excessively drowsy may have sleep apnea rather than ADHD. Treatment for sleep apnea includes removing enlarged tonsils and adenoids or part of the soft palate and dangling uvula at the back of the throat.

Seizure Disorders

Children who have short absence seizures will stare off into space and lose total awareness of their surroundings for a short period of time. Their lack of attention is not an ADD, although seizure disorders may be seen in children with ADHD. Seizure disorders are treated with anticonvulsant medication.

Allergies and Upper Respiratory Illness

Allergies and upper respiratory illnesses can certainly cause a child to be less attentive and on-task in school. Unfortunately, the treatment for allergies may result in side effects that do more harm than good. Both prescription and over-the-counter drugs cause either drowsiness or agitation, both of which make concentration difficult.

Hearing or Vision Problems

Children who have a history of chronic ear infections frequently have a difficult time paying attention in class. Even though they have passed the brief auditory screening at school, one cannot necessarily rule out hearing problems, particularly if the child has a history of frequent ear infections. Congestion in the middle ear can be treated with antihistamines.

Mental Retardation

A child whose intelligence quotient is 70 or below may be identified in schools as mentally impaired. Problems of attention to task may be the result of mental retardation. However, a mentally impaired student may well have ADHD that is not the result of retardation.

Environmental Conditions That May Create Symptoms Similar to ADHD

There are numerous family and societal conditions that can create symptoms in children that might appear to be those of ADHD. These include but are not limited to poor parenting skills; alcoholism; domestic violence; sexual, emotional, or physical abuse; neglect; lack of adult supervision (latchkey kids); dysfunctional and chaotic home environment; split family (child alternates between living with parents who are divorced); parental separation or death; transient living (many moves and lack of stability); parental conflict and lack of agreement on key issues of discipline and child management; or overly high expectations and stress due to pressure to succeed.

These problems do not cause ADHD, but they can of course coexist with ADHD and certainly, when present, will intensify and exacerbate the symptoms of ADHD.

WHAT PROBLEMS FREQUENTLY COEXIST WITH ADHD?

Children with ADHD often have associated conditions and problems that do not warrant a separate diagnosis from ADHD but certainly complicate the evaluation and treatment. These conditions are either a result of the symptoms of ADHD (such as the social skills deficits that grow out of the intrusive-aggressive behavior demonstrated by some children with ADHD), or they frequently exist in common with ADHD (such as immature motor coordination or sleep disturbances). Let me caution you, however, as you read through this laundry list of problems associated with ADHD. You might be tempted to unfairly label at least 50% of the students in your school. Or you could jump to the erroneous conclusion that for a child to have ADHD, he or she would have to have every one of these symptoms. This is not the case. *Not every child with ADHD will exhibit every symptom.* Nor do the symptoms listed here always present themselves in a direct manner. That is the challenge of diagnosing ADHD. Here are some of the most common coexisting conditions.

Academic Performance Problems

Of students with ADHD, 40% to 50% will have diagnosed learning disabilities, and close to 90% will exhibit some type of underachievement in the school setting. Children with ADHD are typically "on" one day and "off" the next. They are consistently inconsistent. Not only do these swings in performance confuse teachers and parents, but they result in the student with ADHD missing a lot of information that other students in the classroom have learned almost effortlessly. Over time, IQ scores of students with ADHD can drop 7 to 15 points because of the cumulative effects of inattention. Many children with ADHD have a difficult time deciding which hand to use for writing, and they may continue to have difficulties with letter reversals and letter sequences into late first and second grade. This makes for difficulties in spelling, reading, and math achievement. They will often depend on finger counting and mnemonic aids longer than most children. To further confound teachers and parents, however, many children with ADHD will be extremely artistic and skilled in mechanical or motor skills outside of formal academic requirements. Their preoccupation with fantasy, imagination, and creative activities may result in elaborate building, drawing, and playing with the superheroes who happen to populate the airwaves at any given point in time. Because children with ADHD have a difficult time learning to tell time and adapting their behavior within time limits, they frequently have problems with time in academic settings (e.g., don't finish work, can't make transitions, or are unaware of the passage of time).

Learning Disabilities

A learning disability as defined by federal law is a disorder in one or more of the basic psychological processes involved in understanding or using language, spoken or written, which may manifest itself in an imperfect ability to listen, think, speak, read, write, spell, or do mathematical calculations. The term does not include children who have learning problems that are primarily the result of visual, hearing, or motor handicaps, of mental retardation, of emotional disturbance, or of environmental, cultural, or economic disadvantage. In layman's language, a learning disability means there is a major discrepancy between a child's ability and performance. Although children with ADHD (without accompanying learning disabilities) often have a large discrepancy between ability and performance, the reasons for this discrepancy are different. Children who are distractible and inattentive will have a hard time learning because of their inattention. But if a child also has a learning disability in association with ADHD, merely getting them on task will not be sufficient. They will still have a problem with the learning task.

Speech and Language Disorders

Children with ADHD are more likely than children in the general population to have speech and language delays and disorders. Problems include delayed onset of talking, linguistic reversals (reversing words in sentences), articulation problems, and expressive inability. Expressive language delays result in limited vocabularies, word-finding difficulties, vague and tangential speech, and poor grammar.

Tourette Syndrome

This is a neurologically based, multiple-tic disorder (motor and vocal tic) that can occur with ADHD. Tourette's syndrome generally includes an involuntary motor tic, such as eye blinking, face twitches, arm or leg movements, hopping, and skipping. The involuntary vocal tics usually involve throat clearing, barks, clicks, grunts, or the uttering of obscenities.[11]

Poor Problem Solving and Organization

Children with ADHD usually tend to have difficulties with complex problem-solving strategies and organizational skills. They also are less efficient in their approach to tasks that require memorization. Their executive command centers seem to shut down when confronted with a large or complex task, and they use impulsive, poorly organized, and inefficient methods to complete a task.

Emotional Reactivity

Children with ADHD often have short fuses. Because of their low frustration tolerance, they are quick to get angry, demonstrate excitement out of proportion to a situation, and overreact to what is happening around them. About 50% of children with ADHD exhibit some symptoms of emotional immaturity, and they are also at higher risk to develop depression as they reach adolescence.

Conduct Problems

Oppositional defiant behavior, temper tantrums, stubbornness, verbal hostility, and angry outbursts characterize children with conduct problems associated with their ADHD. They may be verbally or physically aggressive, lie or steal, and in some cases, even exhibit antisocial and delinquent behavior. Children with ADHD who have associated conduct problems are a challenge to their parents and teachers and need structure and discipline in large doses from a very early age.

Developmental or Medical Problems

Children with ADHD may also exhibit a number of medical problems:

- Delay in gross motor skills (seen in 30%-60% of children with ADHD)
- Delay in fine motor skills, such as handwriting (seen in 60%)
- Greater incidence of enuresis (bed-wetting) (seen in 45%)
- More difficulties with toilet training
- More likely to have accidents (46% are described as accident prone and up to 15% have had at least four or more serious accidents, such as broken bones
- Greater incidence of encopresis (soiling) (seen in 10%)
- Frequent sleep disturbances (seen in 30%)

Social Skills Deficits

Half of the children with ADHD are likely to experience difficulty making and keeping friends. Because they are often selfish and self-centered, they are frequently rejected by their peers. Their lack of awareness of social cues results in immature play and social interests and they exhibit little regard for the social consequences of their behavior.

HOW DOES ADHD AFFECT DAILY LIFE?

Reading about the symptoms and diagnostic criteria of ADHD can't begin to tell the story of how having the disorder, particularly a severe case, will affect the life of a child or adolescent. Taylor, in his book, *Helping Your Hyperactive/ADHD Child,* has assembled a list of mental difficulties, physical challenges, and emotional upheavals that are part of life for and with someone with ADHD.[12]

Among the mental difficulties that Taylor describes are distractibility, confusion, faulty abstract thinking, inflexibility, poor verbal skills, aimlessness, perceptual difficulties (e.g., stumbling, running into things, clumsiness, and awkwardness), and inattention to body states (e.g., not feeling hunger, not feeling pain).

Physical challenges that confront the child or adolescent with ADHD on a daily basis are constant movement, variable rates of development, food cravings, allergies and sensitivities, sleep problems, and coordination problems.

The emotional challenges that are a part of an ADHD diagnosis can keep both child and parent on a veritable roller coaster. Self-centeredness, impatience, recklessness, extreme emotionalism, and a weak conscience are all characteristics that may be observed. The lives of children with ADHD often read like a page from a horror novel or a frame from a bad comedy.

HOW CAN A DEFINITIVE
DIAGNOSIS BE MADE?

A definitive diagnosis of ADHD can only be made by a highly skilled, trained, knowledgeable, and experienced professional. That individual might be a physician, a psychiatrist, or a psychologist.

Often, multidisciplinary teams work together to determine a diagnosis, each member working in his or her own area of expertise. Anyone who works closely with a child can always raise a concern with regard to possible symptoms, but one person alone (even a pediatrician) should not make a definitive diagnosis without consultation and teamwork. The recent trends in managed health care, which allow fewer if any opportunities for self-referral to a specialist, often find the primary care physician prescribing Ritalin™ or some other medication with little or no consultation with school personnel or other health care professionals. Follow-up can often be sporadic and support for the family nonexistent.

IS THERE A CURE FOR ADHD?

No. There are no medications, behavior modification programs, psychotherapy, or counseling programs that will "cure" ADHD. The symptoms will always be a part of a child's life, although they may change or moderate as he or she gets older. But the symptoms must constantly be acknowledged and managed. Medication, behavior management programs, counseling, parent training, and school interventions will in many cases diminish the impact that ADHD symptoms can have on school success, social relationships, and ultimate achievement and satisfaction as an adult. But, early intervention and cooperative home-school relationships are critically important.

NOTES

1. Thomas Armstrong. *The Myth of the A.D.D. Child*. New York: Dutton, 1995, p. xii.

2. Thom Hartmann. *Attention Deficit Disorder: A Different Perception*. Novato, California: Underwood-Miller, 1993.

3. Peter Schrag and Diane Divoky. *The Myth of the Hyperactive Child and Other Means of Child Control*. New York: Pantheon, 1975.

Alfie Kohn. "Suffer the Restless Children." *Atlantic Monthly*, November, 1989, 264, p. 90.

5. Reprinted with permission from the American Psychiatric Association's *Diagnostic and Statistical Manual of Mental Disorders*, Fourth Edition, pp. 83-85. Washington, DC: American Psychiatric Association, 1994.

6.   Allan Zametkin et al. "Cerebral Glucose Metabolism in Adults with Hyperactivity of Childhood Onset." *New England Journal of Medicine*, 1990, 323, pp. 1361-1366.

7.   Xavier Castellanos, et al. "Quantitative Brain Magnetic Resonance Imaging in ADHD," *Archives of General Psychiatry*, July, 1996, 53, pp. 607-616.

8.   Russell A. Barkley. *Attention Deficit Hyperactivity Disorder: A Handbook for Diagnosis and Treatment.* New York: The Guilford Press, 1990, p. 99.

9.   Russell A. Barkley. *ADHD: What Can We Do?* Program Manual for Video. New York: Guilford Publications, Inc., 1992, p. 5.

10.   Russell A. Barkley. *Attention Deficit Hyperactivity Disorder: A Handbook for Diagnosis and Treatment,* op. cit., p. 100.

11.   Utah State Office of Education. "The Relationship of Attention Deficit Disorder to Other Conditions." *The Utah Attention Deficit Disorder Guide,* pp. 8-10. Salt Lake City, UT: Utah State Office of Education, 1994.

12.   John F. Taylor. *The Hyperactive Child and the Family: The Complete What-to-do Handbook.* New York: Everest House, 1980, pp. 15-27.

2

THE RULES AND REGS

What Does the Law Say About ADHD?

Our school personnel have really been terrific. We work as a team to handle problems and devise solutions. I provide teachers with ADHD reading material on an ongoing basis and keep very much in touch with them along the way.

—Vivian Martineli

Until this year [freshman year in high school], the schools and teachers have made life hell for us. We have encountered stubborn ignorance and very unprofessional attitudes. Educators have exacerbated the problem to the point of our despair. Thank goodness we've found an administration that has knowledge of ADD and a true desire to help the student.

—Karen Beacon

Public schools have the responsibility to educate every student, but specific legislative rules and regulations govern the education of students with disabilities and special learning needs. As an educator, you cannot afford to plead ignorance, lack of money, parental irresponsibility, or lack of materials or training when it comes to meeting the needs of students with ADHD. Here is what the law has to say.

WHAT DOES THE LAW SAY ABOUT
SERVING STUDENTS WITH ADHD?

There are three separate federal laws that govern the decisions to be made regarding the provision of services to meet the needs of students with ADHD. These are (a) the Individuals with Disabilities Act, Part B (IDEA); (b) Section 504 of the Rehabilitation Act of 1973; and (c) the Americans with Disabilities Act (ADA).

IDEA

The Individuals with Disabilities Act (IDEA, PL 101-476), formerly the Education of the Handicapped Act (P.L. 94-142, passed in 1975), authorizes and funds special education services. In 1990, when Congress was considering the reauthorization of IDEA, they debated including ADHD as a separate disability category. This would have made students with ADHD eligible for special education services solely on the basis of their ADHD. However, Congress decided, on the recommendation of the U.S. Education Department, that because many students with ADHD were already eligible for special services by virtue of coexisting disabilities, they would not create a separate category. At the time of this decision, Congress directed the Education Department to solicit comments regarding how students with ADHD were then being served in the public schools. The department received over 2,000 comments from individuals regarding this issue and on September 16, 1991 issued a Policy Memorandum, signed by three Department Assistant Secretaries, expressly recognizing students with ADHD as eligible for special education and related services under federal law. The policy makes clear that students with ADHD qualify for special education and related services solely on the basis of ADHD, when the ADHD itself impairs educational performance or learning, under both (a) Public Law 101-476, Individuals with Disabilities Act (IDEA) Part B "other health impaired" statutes and regulations, and (b) Section 504 of the 1973 Rehabilitation Act plus its implementing regulations. This departmental policy statement did not define ADHD as a new disability category but rather, confirmed and elaborated that ADHD was a disability already covered by existing law (see Appendix C).

An additional memo from the Office of Civil Rights (OCR) issued in early 1993 (see Appendix D) and clarified again in 1994 (see Appendix E), addressed in detail OCR's position on evaluation and identification, as well as school districts' responsibilities with regard to students with ADHD. These three documents are important reading in order to understand your legal responsibilities with respect to students with ADHD and their parents.

To summarize, to receive special education services, a student with ADHD must undergo an evaluation conducted by the school district and be found to have either

1. one or more of the 13 disabilities specified in the IDEA or
2. impaired educational performance or learning under IDEA (Part B) "other health impaired" statutes and regulations.

Among the 13 categories specified in the IDEA into which many students with ADHD fall, two are learning disabilities and serious emotional disturbances. The federal definition of a learning disability is as follows:

A disorder in one or more of the basic psychological processes involved in understanding or in using language, spoken or written, that may manifest itself in an imperfect ability to listen, think, read, write, spell, or do mathematical calculations. The term [learning disabilities] includes such conditions as perceptual disabilities, brain injury, minimal brain dysfunction, dyslexia, and developmental aphasia. The term does not apply to students who have learning problems that are primarily the result of visual, hearing, or motor disabilities, of mental retardation, of emotional disturbance, or of environmental, cultural, or economic disadvantage.[1]

A student will be labeled as learning disabled only if he or she does not perform in school on a level with his or her peers in the areas of oral expression, listening comprehension, written expression, reading comprehension, mathematical reasoning, and mathematical calculation but is shown to have the ability to do so.

A second disability category (of the 13 listed in IDEA) under which many students with ADHD are qualified to receive special education services is Emotionally Disturbed. An emotional disturbance is defined by the Federal Government as follows:

1. An inability to learn, which cannot be explained by intellectual, sensory, or health factors

2. An inability to build or maintain satisfactory interpersonal relationships with peers and teachers
3. Inappropriate types of behavior or feelings under normal circumstances
4. A general pervasive mood of unhappiness or depression
5. A tendency to develop physical symptoms or fears associated with personal or school problems

The term *emotionally disturbed* includes schizophrenia. The term does not apply to students who are socially maladjusted, unless it is determined that they have a serious emotional disturbance.[2]

One other disability of the 13 listed in IDEA, and cited earlier as the second way to access special education services, is the "other health impaired" category. This category, commonly referred to as *Part B*, includes all chronic (longstanding) or acute (recent onset) impairments that result in limited alertness that adversely affects educational performance. Under this category, a student with diagnosed ADHD may be eligible for special education services without having any other disability (such as a learning disability or an emotional impairment). Questions have arisen with regard to whether the diagnosis of ADHD for eligibility under Part B must be made by a licensed physician. If your school district believes that a medical evaluation is a necessary prerequisite for identifying a student as needing services because he or she has ADHD and specifically recommends such an evaluation to the parent, the district must bear the cost of this evaluation.

> However, if the school district believes that other effective means of measuring ADD are available, then qualified personnel other than licensed physicians may be used to conduct the evaluation, so long as all of the evaluation requirements under Regs. 300.530-300.534 are met."[3]

These regulations stipulate that a multidisciplinary team must participate in the evaluation, and at least one individual on the team must be knowledgeable about the possible adverse effects of ADHD on a student's school performance.

Section 504

The second federal law that governs decisions to be made regarding the provision of services to meet the needs of students with ADHD is Section 504 of the Rehabilitation Act of 1973. Section 504 is not a special education law that provides federal funding to facilitate special education programs and services. Rather, it is a civil rights statute that prohibits discrimination on the basis of handicap. The law applies to any entity that receives federal financial assistance and thus applies to every public school district. Although there are no federal funds flowing from Section 504, failure to comply with its requirements will result in the withdrawal of federal funds.

A student who does not qualify for special education services because of a specific disability or a health impairment under IDEA may be eligible for services under Section 504. As defined in Section 504 regulations, a "person with a disability" is any person who has a physical or mental impairment substantially limiting a major life activity, such as learning, has a record of such an impairment, or is regarded as having such an impairment.

Many students with ADHD do not need to be formally labeled or receive any type of special services if they are managing the academic and social demands of school with no problems. Where disagreements and conflicts between parents and school officials can often occur, however, is when parents are convinced that a label and special education services are necessary, and school personnel do not reach that conclusion. At issue is the definition of "school success." Gifted students with ADHD often "fall through the cracks" because their grades hover in the "C" range. Although these average (and to many teachers and administrators, acceptable) grades may not raise a red flag or produce the kind of teacher referral that failing grades and severe behavioral problems may generate, they clearly represent a discrepancy between ability and achievement that deserves intervention and accommodation. No matter how severe a student's difficulties, the least restrictive approach to meeting a student's needs should always be preferred. Labeling a student serves no purpose if he or she is being well-served without any labels. However, if a student is not succeeding in school and is having severe academic and social problems, that student must be evaluated, and, if found eligible, be serviced. Remember that a medical diagnosis of ADHD alone does not guarantee eligibility for either special education or 504 services. Parents are often confused on this issue, but the law is very clear. The law also states that a school district cannot refuse to evaluate a student because he or she has already received a medical diagnosis of ADHD.

A formal individualized education plan (IEP), a document required if a student receives special education services under IDEA, is not mandated under Section 504, but developing an IEP and offering special education services *would* be one way of meeting the free appropriate public education requirement of Section 504.

The September 16, 1991, memo issued by the Education Department suggests that the guidelines could be met by

> providing a structured learning environment; repeating and simplifying instructions about in-class and homework assignments; supplementing verbal instructions with visual instructions; using behavioral management techniques; adjusting class schedules; modifying test delivery; using tape recorders, computer-aided instruction, and other audiovisual equipment; selecting modified textbooks or workbooks; and tailoring homework assignments. (See Appendix C)

Other modifications suggested by the federal government include (a) consultation services; (b) reduction of class size; (c) use of one-on-one tutorials, classroom aides, and note takers; (d) involvement of a "service coordinator" to oversee implementation of special programs and services; and (e) possible modifications of nonacademic times, such as lunchroom, recess, and physical education. Wherever possible, these interventions should occur in the regular classroom environment.

An evaluation for eligibility under Section 504 has not been defined and structured for practitioners like an evaluation under IDEA. Under Section 504, there are no eligibility categories, no checklists for eligibility criteria, and no rules as to who should conduct the evaluation other than a generalized statement that tests and other evaluation material must be administered by trained personnel in conformance with the instructions provided by their producer. Similar to Part B, however, under Section 504, a school district must draw on information from a variety of sources. Under Section 504, these sources include, but are not limited to, aptitude and achievement tests, teacher recommendations, physical condition, social or cultural background, and adaptive behavior. Although Section 504 does not specify a multidisciplinary evaluation team or discuss IEPs, the law does require that placement decisions be made by a group of persons that shall include persons knowledgeable about the student, the meaning of the evaluation data, and placement options. Appendix J contains sample policies that should be in place in every school district to cover the implementation of Section 504. Chapter 3 discusses in detail the evaluation process and offers a variety of forms and procedures for conducting a 504 evaluation in accordance with the policies shown in Appendix J.

Title II and Title III of the
Americans with Disabilities Act (ADA)

The ADA is the third law that could conceivably affect the educational status of students with ADHD. Titles II and III of the ADA went into effect on January 26, 1992. Title II of the ADA applies to all local government entities, including local and intermediate school districts, whether or not these entities receive federal financial assistance. Title III of the ADA applies to public accommodations, which include private but *not* parochial schools. Both Titles II and III are intended to provide protection to individuals with disabilities that is at least as great as that provided under Section 504. Because the ADA regulations do not address issues such as evaluation or a student's rights to a free appropriate public education (FAPE), there is little likelihood that this civil rights statute, which expands Section 504 from the public to the private sector, will supplant IDEA-Part B and Section 504 as the defining parameters for the specific educational rights of students with ADHD.

WHAT ARE THE
SERVICE DELIVERY OPTIONS?

There is a wide range of service options to be considered, from least restrictive to most restrictive, when deciding how to best meet the needs of a student with ADHD. Least restrictive, in educational terms, means that the option provides all services within the regular classroom setting. The most restrictive option removes the student from the regular education classroom, possibly even to a self-contained placement in another school or a private out-of-district placement. Private or parochial and home-schooling options are also included in the continuum because some parents will elect these alternatives.

Public School Options

1. If a student with ADHD has not been formally identified as needing special education services under IDEA or services under Section 504 of the Rehabilitation Act of 1973 through a formal case study evaluation or Section 504 evaluation, all services will be provided in the regular classroom by the classroom teacher with no formal paperwork or support services.

Advantages

* No label has been attached to the student.
* No special education records are developed.
* Student will not leave the classroom and be separated from his or her peer group.

Disadvantages

* Continuity and level of services depends solely on the skill and cooperation of regular education teachers.
* Plan is informal and will need extensive monitoring and support from parents.
* Level of service may be insufficient to keep the student from receiving mediocre if not failing grades in many academic subjects.

2. If a student with ADHD has been determined to be eligible for services under Section 504 of the Rehabilitation Act of 1973, services are provided in the regular public school classroom with support from the teacher assistance team and a 504 Plan (see Figure 3.17, Chapter 3).

Advantages

* Student is labeled as ADHD, but no special education label is placed on the student.
* An IEP or 504 plan will be developed for the student, but no special education records are kept and no labels are entered into the student's school records.
* Services are provided for the student as needed.

Disadvantages

* Teachers and administrators may need special training to successfully implement the plan.
* The level of services may not be adequate to meet the needs of the student.

3. If a student with ADHD has been determined to be eligible for services under IDEA and has been labeled as learning disabled, emotionally disturbed, or other health impaired, all services can be pro-

vided in the regular education classroom with support for student and teacher, even for those students with very severe disabilities. This program, known as *inclusive education,* is being implemented in many school districts across the country.

Advantages

- An IEP is developed.
- Clearly defined legal rights for the parent and student are spelled out.
- All services are provided within the context of the regular classroom (inclusive education). Depending on the needs of the student, a resource teacher, one-to-one aide, inclusion facilitator, or other personnel will assist the regular classroom teacher in modifying the curriculum and assignments and assisting the student.
- Students are not pulled out of their regular classroom or placed exclusively in a so-called self-contained classroom where they will only interact with students who have disabilities similar to theirs.

Disadvantages

- For the student with severe disabilities, this service option offers no major disadvantages. The success of this service option does depend, however, on the complete support and cooperation of parent, classroom teacher, administrator, central office personnel, and the Board of Education.
- Parents of other students may apply pressure to teachers and administrator when a student with ADHD "diverts" teacher time from their students. Although this is not a disadvantage to the student, administrators will need to be prepared to handle this aspect of inclusive education.

4. If a student has been determined to be eligible for services under IDEA and has been labeled as learning disabled, emotionally disturbed, or other health impaired, services may be provided in the regular education classroom as well as in a setting called the *resource room.* The student will be served by a regular classroom teacher and a special education resource teacher.

Advantages

* An IEP is developed.
* Clearly defined legal rights for parent and student are spelled out.
* Student spends a portion of the day in the regular classroom and has the benefit of peer role models and social opportunities.
* Student receives special help that is geared to his or her needs.

Disadvantages

* Student is pulled out to receive support services of a resource teacher or other personnel. Although the special help is usually beneficial, the student is clearly labeled as different and misses activities in the regular classroom whenever he or she leaves.

5. If a student has been determined to be eligible for services under IDEA and has been labeled as learning disabled, emotionally disturbed, or other health impaired, services might be provided in a self-contained classroom located in a regular public school. A student could be "mainstreamed," integrated in the regular classroom for his or her grade level, for some subjects, but he or she would spend the majority of the day in the self-contained classroom with students who have similar disabilities.

Advantages

* Teacher-to-student ratio is maximized.
* Special programming, such as the use of classified token economies or assigning points for acceptable behavior, can take place.
* The pace and organization of the self-contained classroom provides for as few interruptions and transitions as possible, maximizing learning time and minimizing opportunities for off-task behavior.
* Students work with the same teachers and can develop a routine.

Disadvantages

* Costly method for school district.
* No suitable peer role models for students with disabilities.
* Student may not attend his or her "home-neighborhood" school.
* Very restrictive environment for students.

6. If a student has been determined to be eligible for services under IDEA and has been labeled as learning disabled, emotionally disturbed, or other health impaired, services might be provided in a self-contained special education class on a campus containing only special education classes or sent to a residential private placement. Decisions to place students in these settings are made based on severity of the disability.

Advantages

* Student who would be incapable of receiving an education elsewhere has an educational option.

Disadvantages

* Severely restrictive.
* Very costly.
* No suitable peer role models for students.

Private, Parochial, or Home School Options

1. Regardless of whether a student has been identified as needing special education services under IDEA or services under Section 504 through a formal case study evaluation or 504 evaluation, a parent may choose to enroll the student in a private or parochial school placement.

Advantages

* No label is attached to the student.
* No special education records are developed.
* Student will not leave the classroom and be separated from his peer group.
* Teacher-pupil ratios may be better.

Disadvantages

* Teachers may lack techniques and expertise to meet needs of student.
* Private school budgets don't always permit the extra staff training that is needed to successfully work with students who have ADHD.

- Support staff to train and advise teachers is often minimal to nonexistent.

- Parents of other students may apply pressure to teachers and administrator when a student with ADHD diverts teacher time from their students.

- Cost to parents may be substantial.

2. Regardless of whether a student has been identified as needing special education services under IDEA or services under Section 504 through a formal case study evaluation or 504 evaluation, the parent(s) may choose to enroll the student in a parent-funded special school for students with ADHD.

Advantages

- Teacher-pupil ratios may be better.

- School may be connected to a university or hospital where access to up-to-date research and methodology is available.

Disadvantages

- Although the student may not be officially labeled, by reason of attending a special school, the label will be inherent.

- Services may not be as complete as in public settings because funding is often completely dependent on tuition and endowments.

- Cost to parents may be substantial.

3. Regardless of whether a student has been identified as needing special education services under IDEA or services under Section 504 through a formal case study evaluation or 504 evaluation, the parent(s) may choose to enroll the student in a parent-funded military or structured boarding school.

Advantages

- Structure with expectations and consequences are provided.

- Predictable, daily routine is provided.

- Tight external controls help some students control their anti-social tendencies.

Disadvantages

- Costly to parents.
- Rigid rules and inflexibility may exacerbate inability to sustain attention on long tasks.
- Conflict with authority may occur with students who have conduct or oppositional problems.

4. Regardless of whether a student has been identified as needing special education services under IDEA or services under Section 504 through a formal case study evaluation or 504 evaluation, the parent(s) may choose to home school the student.

Advantages

- Individual attention can be provided.
- Home-school friction can be eliminated.
- Learning program can be tailored to student's learning style.

Disadvantages

- Dual role of teacher-parent can be exhausting when working with students with ADHD.
- Parent may lack the skill needed to modify curriculum.
- Student who needs social skills training and opportunities will have few options in the home school setting and may risk long-term social problems.

WHAT LEGAL RIGHTS DO PARENTS HAVE?

There are many actions that a parent can take under the law if he or she is not satisfied with a student's educational program.[4] Parents might

- request a psychoeducational evaluation to determine if a student qualifies for special education under IDEA.
- submit a copy of any documentation supporting a diagnosis of ADHD.
- request that the evaluation also consider eligibility under Section 504 if the student is not eligible under IDEA.

- contact the district's compliance officer to discuss concerns if the school district does not agree to evaluate for eligibility under Section 504.

- file a complaint with the U.S. Office for Civil Rights (see Appendix E) if the district ultimately refuses to evaluate for eligibility under Section 504.

If a student with ADHD is receiving special education services but the IEP doesn't address his or her needs related to ADHD, the parent can

- request a staffing to review the IEP and request specific changes necessary to address the ADHD (e.g., counseling or modified assignments).

- write his or her disagreement on the IEP and sign it if changes cannot be agreed on.

- request written notice for each refusal.

- contact the district's compliance officer and discuss concerns about the educational needs related to ADHD.

- request mediation (voluntary) or due process hearing or file a complaint with the OCR (see Appendix B for a list of district OCRs and Appendix E for the OCR's official position on ADHD).

If a student has been diagnosed with ADHD and is determined not to be eligible for special education but is eligible under Section 504, a parent may

- request that a written plan be developed that will include the appropriate program to be provided by the district.

- urge the district to include the following components in the written plan as are found in the IEP: a statement of the present level of educational performance; annual goals and short-term instructional objectives; specific special education, if any, and related services; objective criteria for measuring educational progress; and academic modifications.

- indicate the disagreement in writing if the district refuses to include necessary academic modifications, related services, or other necessary programs.

- request a copy of the school's procedural safeguards under Section 504.

If a student with ADHD has a written plan under Section 504 that is appropriate, but is not being followed by the school district, the parent may file a complaint with the U.S. Office for Civil Rights. For a comprehensive statement of parental rights granted by federal law for students with handicaps, see Appendix H.

HOW DOES INCLUSIVE EDUCATION AFFECT STUDENTS WITH ADHD?

Although we have come a long way since 1975 when Public Law 94-142, the Education for All Handicapped Children Act, was passed, the inclusion of all (or most) students with disabilities in the regular classroom, with support help for both students and teachers, is not a widespread reality. The exclusionary policies that were common before the passage of 94-142 resulted in more than a million children and young people with disabilities being totally excluded from the public schools of the United States. And although those inequalities have been addressed for the most part, educational practices have largely focused on creating special self-contained classes or pull-out tutorial services. Although the student is receiving educational services, he or she is separated and isolated from peers and the mainstream of school life. Public Law 94-142 gave rights to students with disabilities and their parents or guardians. These rights are worth rereading as you consider the inequity implied in the total isolation of students with disabilities:

- The right to a free appropriate public education, with all necessary supportive services, for all young people between the ages of 5 and 21 years, no matter what their disability. *All students will be served.*

- The right to be fairly tested and evaluated by a team of professionals. The law requires that schools and other agencies must give tests to students that show both their strengths and weaknesses. All tests must be given to students in their own language and in such a way that their abilities and their disabilities are accurately displayed.

- The right to receive this education in the least restrictive environment possible for each student, to discourage both the practice of segregating students with disabilities from others ("because it's better for them") and the perception of educating the disability rather than the student. Students are to be educated in a separate classroom or school only when the nature and the severity of their disabilities makes it impossible to meet their educational needs in a less restrictive environment.

* The right to an IEP for each student, listing specific educational goals and objectives along with a timetable for them, with a proviso that the IEP be reviewed at least once a year. Parent participation in the evolution of the student's IEP has been termed the core element of the law. A student has a right to a full range of educational services, which may include such related services as special transportation, speech-language therapy, counseling, occupational or physical therapy, or other services necessary to enable him or her to benefit from special education.

* The right, in the case of parent dissatisfaction with the school's implementation of the law, to an impartial due process procedure, a series of steps available for parents to appeal against evaluations, placement decisions, or programs with which they disagreed, or against failure by the school to provide related services necessary for the student to benefit from the other rights.

NOTES

1. Public Law 102-119, 20 USC 1401[a][1].

2. Ibid.

3. *Individuals with Disabilities Education Law Report*, 18(19). Horsham, PA: LRP Publications, 1992.

4. Arizona Council for Children with Attention Deficit Disorders. *Attention Deficit Disorder: A Parent's Guide.* Tucson, Arizona: Arizona Council for Children with Attention Deficit Disorders, 1992, p. 16.

3

EVALUATING ATTENTIONAL CONCERNS

How to Determine if a Student Has ADHD

I've Got A Wiggle in My Brain

I've got a wiggle in my brain
And I think I'll go insane
Cause I just can't stop
The wiggle in my brain,
Or in my knees,
Or in my feet,
Or in my toe,
Oh no!
　　　　—Parody of Joe Scruggs's song
　　　　"There's a Wiggle in My Toe"
　　　　　　by Daniel Burns,
　　　a six-year-old boy with ADHD

Professional educators sometimes describe their ability to recognize ADHD similarly to the way in which Supreme Court Justice Potter Stewart described his methodology for identifying pornography—"I know it when I see it."[1] There are, however, a number of factors that make this approach to evaluating ADHD a particularly risky one.

- There are no federal or state-regulated criteria for identifying ADHD such as exist for learning or other disabilities. The closest we can come to an official governmental definition has been issued by the OCR.[2] So nailing down just exactly whether ADHD is present or not is a job for a team of experts, not just one teacher or principal.

- The presenting symptoms of ADHD can often occur in conjunction with other medical or psychological problems.

- The presenting symptoms of ADHD are regularly seen in the average student who does not have ADHD (although usually not in the same quantity and intensity).

- Because the diagnosis of ADHD depends largely on interviews and behavioral rating scales, the bias of the individuals completing the rating scale can sometimes skew the results.

- The symptoms of ADHD are variable. Students will present one set of symptoms and behavior in one setting and act much differently in another.

- Although the most dramatic symptoms of ADHD, such as oppositional defiant behavior and extreme hyperactivity (I call it the "Dennis the Menace syndrome"), are easy to spot, there are many students (especially girls) who fall through the cracks because no one gets excited about what usually appears to be daydreaming, the "social butterfly syndrome," or "spaciness."

- Last, making a casual remark to a parent that his or her child may have ADHD and should be on medication could make your district liable for the costs of a medical evaluation.

WHO SHOULD DIAGNOSE ADHD?

Depending on where the concerns have arisen regarding a student's behavior, academic performance, or both, there are many individuals who will play a part in a thorough diagnostic evaluation. Each participant in the process will be able to reveal or uncover different aspects of a student's behavior, social skills, personality, medical status, and academic skills. Although all of the individuals who are described in the following discussion may not be consulted in every evaluation, each one has an important role to play in both the diagnostic and treatment phases of a student's evaluation.

Parents' Role

The parents' role in the diagnostic process is a crucial one. Because they have been observing and informally assessing their child since birth, they have quantities of information about their child's academic and behavioral strengths and weaknesses as well as the child's concerns about school and home. A skillfully managed interview combined with the results of standardized rating scales can usually elicit an objective picture of both the student and his or her home setting.

Student's Role

The student may sometimes be the primary catalyst for seeking professional help. Sue and Charles Kingman knew their son Brent was different, but his problems at school weren't that serious. He did always seem to be in trouble with his two older siblings at home, but that was chalked up to his being the youngest. Even when he complained about nobody liking him because he was a brat, his parents didn't pay too much attention to his whining. But his statement that when he got older, he was going to kill himself definitely made mom and dad take notice. They began to take seriously his problems with self-esteem at home and school. They realized that he was crying out for help. They immediately made an appointment with a child psychologist for an evaluation. ADHD was determined to be the diagnosis.

Teacher's Role

The teacher has a unique opportunity to observe the student in both academic and social settings. He or she knows the student's learning strengths and weaknesses and will have some suggestions about which behavior management and instructional techniques have been most successful.

Principal's Role

As a key player in all of the decisions that are made about the students in your school, you will probably already have some information about the student who is being referred. He or she may have been to visit you in your office about a disciplinary matter. Or you may have signed an interim report that notified his or her parents of academic concerns. The parents may even have called your office to talk about their concerns with the teacher's effectiveness. Your role should be one of facilitator and communicator as you provide support and encouragement for all of the players in the screening and evaluation process. Meeting the needs of students with ADHD can be stressful and frustrating for everyone involved. You can provide a shoulder to cry on.

School Psychologist's Role

The school psychologist can provide consultation and support to the teacher, help the parents understand the school's strengths and limitations in meeting the needs of the student, and provide educational information to the teachers and parents. The school psychologist may also administer intellectual and academic performance testing if it is recommended by the child study team or student support team. School psychologists frequently have expertise in the areas of learning disabilities, behavior management, classroom management strategies, social skills training, brain dominance, and learning-style preference.

Behavior Management Specialist's Role

The behavior management specialist is skilled at working with classroom teachers, parents, and students to develop behavior management plans. He or she is trained to observe students in classroom settings and monitor their on-task behavior. He or she can often provide training for the student in self-monitoring of behavior as well as in social skill development.

School Social Worker or Counselor's Role

The school social worker or counselor may have information about the student's perceptions gained through counseling sessions that is not available from any other professional. Students who are experiencing school adjustment problems are frequently referred to the social worker or counselor.

Physician's Role

The family physician or pediatrician will often meet with parents alone to discuss concerns and review information, obtain a thorough medical history, review the developmental and school history, and review the family's medical, learning, and attending problems. The physician might also meet with the student alone (depending on age) to review concerns and solicit his or her views of problems at home and school. During this time, the physician might also informally assess the student's social and emotional status. A thorough physical exam will then be administered, including a vision and hearing screening and blood tests that usually include a chemical profile and thyroid functioning test (to rule out any medical reasons for symptoms). As appropriate, the physician might refer to the neurologist; ophthalmologist; an ear, nose, and throat (ENT) specialist; allergist; psychologist; learning disability specialist; speech and language pathologist; family therapist; social worker; or an occupational or physical therapist.

Child Psychologist's Role

The child psychologist will evaluate the student thoroughly for psychological and emotional problems; intellectual strengths and weaknesses; educational deficits; attention, concentration, and impulse control; family relationships; and peer-social relationships.

Child Psychiatrist's Role

The child psychiatrist will assist other professionals in differentiating the diagnosis of ADHD from other psychiatric disorders, such as oppositional defiant disorder, conduct disorder, depression, bipolar disorder, and thought disorder. The child psychiatrist might treat for severe emotional problems that coexist with the attention disorders. The child psychiatrist will become involved if hospitalization is necessary because of severe depression or unmanageable behavior.

Neurologist's Role

The neurologist will rule out seizure disorders, including complex partial seizures or narcolepsy as contributing factors. He or she will recommend electroencephalogram (EEG) evaluations if indicated.

Allergist's Role

The allergist will determine the presence of allergies, asthma, and food intolerances and treat any problems found.

Ear, Nose, and Throat Specialist's Role

The ENT specialist will evaluate hearing and middle-ear fluid problems if the student has a history of chronic ear infections. He or she will be aware of auditory processing problems and language-based learning disabilities sometimes resulting from chronic ear infections.

Ophthalmologist's Role

The ophthalmologist will evaluate vision, visual perception, and depth perception thoroughly, especially when the student has problems with blurring words, slow copying from the board, reading problems, family history of vision problems, and clumsiness or poor coordination. The ophthalmologist will then treat any visual problems diagnosed.

Family Therapist-Social Worker's Role

The family therapist-social worker will educate parents on ADHD and its effect on the family and assist the family in treating any dysfunctional interactions. This individual may also provide psychotherapy for the student or parents or both together.

WHAT STEPS SHOULD BE FOLLOWED IN ADDRESSING ATTENTIONAL CONCERNS?

Attentional concerns about a student can come from anyone, but the individuals on the direct firing line with a student—parents and teachers—are usually the first to raise the red flag of warning. Note the use of the phrase, "attentional concerns," in the context of the school setting. Although this term may seem somewhat euphemistic, until there is a definitive diagnosis by a health care professional, the red flag on the part of educators only signifies concerns, not a full-blown diagnosis. Educators cannot and should not attempt to make a medical diagnosis of ADHD.

Attentional concerns raised at school usually fall into one of the following categories:

- Starting tasks
- Staying on task
- Completing tasks
- Making transitions
- Interacting with others
- Following through on directions
- Producing work at consistently normal levels
- Organizing multistep tasks.[3]

Home problems will frequently relate to sibling relationships, self-esteem, following rules, social relationships in the neighborhood, and hyperactive behavior. The parents' investigation of ADHD as a possible diagnosis (if possible, undertaken on their own initiative and at their own expense) may proceed independently or simultaneously with that of the school's.

Decisions about how to meet the needs of a student with ADHD are best made in the team setting using a standardized process. Many districts across the country have developed a districtwide assessment procedure similar to the Attentional Concerns Flowchart illustrated in Figure 3.1 and described in detail in the following sections. The process provides ample opportunity for interventions, discussions, and collaboration of the professional staff in your building, enabling your team to reach the best possible educational decision regarding a student's needs while also fulfilling the important legal requirements that were addressed in Chapter Two. As you read through the steps of this process, consult Figure 3.1 as well as the many sample forms and checklists that are a part of gathering information and making decisions.

Step 1

If attentional concerns are noted by a parent or school staff member, modifications should be made immediately within the student's classroom to assist the student to improve his or her attending skills. Teachers should, of course, always keep the parents informed about the various modifications or interventions that are being attempted. Under no circumstances should a teacher or principal recommend a medical evaluation, allude to the possibility of ADHD, or suggest to a parent that a child would benefit from medication. Alert your staff members to the importance of discretion in this matter. The ADHD Intervention Checklist (see Form 5.1 in Chapter Five) will prove invaluable in considering which strategies will be most beneficial for the student. The checklist will also provide an ongoing documentation record of the success or failure of the attempted interventions.

Step 2

If the modifications and interventions attempted by the classroom teacher are not sufficiently successful in improving the student's classroom functioning, the teacher may request a consultation meeting with the building's teacher assistance team (TAT) or PPS (pupil personnel services) team using forms similar to those shown in Forms 3.1 and 3.2. The classroom teacher (or other designated person) is also responsible for asking the appropriate health staff (health aide or school nurse) to complete a vision and hearing screening prior to the informational meeting. Ruling out possible hearing and vision problems before proceeding to the next step is extremely important because these difficulties can sometimes result in attention difficulties and academic failure. For students who have had previous vision and hearing screenings, the health staff will determine whether or not a new screening is necessary.

Step 3

Schedule the TAT or PPS informational meeting and review the intervention data. Ask teachers to come to the meeting with written documentation of interventions that have been attempted using the ADHD Intervention Checklist (Form 5.1 in Chapter Five). Review each intervention attempted, the date of initiation, date(s) of modification(s), and the level of success. A minimum of 15 school days of implementation should be documented for each intervention-modification. The classroom teacher and the TAT or PPS team should then determine which additional interventions may be appropriate and set time lines for review. A case manager will be assigned by the building TAT or PPS team. Although parent conferences have undoubtedly already been held, and parents may even have attended the informational meeting, at this time, a letter will be sent to parents constituting an official written notification of attentional concerns. Although this letter in no way recommends that parents seek medical advice, it does offer the cooperation of school personnel should parents choose to do so (see Form 3.3).

Step 4

If the TAT or PPS team determines that the data indicates a need to pursue an ADHD screening, secure parent permission using the Attentional Concerns Screening Permission Form (Form 3.4). Although parental permission is not a legal requirement (except in the case of the student interview), parents should be kept informed at each step of the process and use of this form will insure that parents are aware of what is happening. Permission for the screening will be secured by the classroom teacher. As soon as the permission is received, the classroom teacher will notify the case manager and the screening will begin. If the parent indicates a desire for more information before consent is given, the case manager will be responsible for contacting the parent and answering any questions. The screening should include but not necessarily be limited to the following areas:

Direct Observation of Behavior Across Settings

Although assessment instruments can provide a wealth of information, there is no substitute for observing the child in his or her natural setting. Students with ADHD may well be model students in a one-on-one situation, so observing these students in more typical settings is especially important. Information that might be noted includes the position of the student's desk, the amount of contact with the teacher, the length of the assignments, the instructional mode (e.g., lecture, small group work), possible auditory and visual distracters, degree and frequency of peer interaction, student's response to behavioral management program, severity of problems, student's method of organization of materials and activities, the student's ability to transition from one activity to another, the methods used by the teacher to inform the student about his or her daily routine and schedule, the amount of work completed by the student as compared to peers, and the degree of difficulties in structured classroom settings versus nonstructured settings, such as lunchroom or recess. (See Appendix F for behavior observation instructions that explain in detail how to objectively assess a student's classroom behavior using the sample forms shown in Forms 3.5 and 3.6). Either the school psychologist, social worker, behavioral management specialist, or a teacher assistant who has been trained in behavioral observation might complete this aspect of the screening.

Parent Questionnaires and Rating Scales

There are two types of parent rating scales: those that report on the child and those that are completed by the parents regarding their own practices. Some examples of child rating scales include the Child Behavior Checklist (Achenbach & Edelbrock, 1991), Conners Parent Rating Scale-Revised (Goyette, Conners, & Ulrich, 1978), Home Situations Questionnaire-Revised (DuPaul & Barkley, 1990), and Attention Deficit Disorders Evaluation Scale, Home Version (McCarney, 1989).

Russell Barkley believes that parent self-report scales are almost as important in the evaluation of students with ADHD as those completed by parents and teachers about the students. The Locke-Wallace Marital Adjustment Test is a commonly used brief rating scale of marital satisfaction. Marital difficulties may result in greater problems in child management and affect the willingness of a couple to receive training. Two additional instruments that gather information about parents are the Parenting Stress Index and the Parenting Practices Scale. The Home Situations Questionnaire-Revised shown in Form 3.7 was developed by Russell A. Barkley and is widely used with students aged 4 to 18 years to evaluate specific problems with attention and concentration across a variety of home and public situations. Sample items from another more recently developed parent rating scale, the ACTeRS Parent Form, are shown in Form 3.9.

Teacher Questionnaires and Rating Scales

Those teachers who have worked with students for longer periods of time will of course give more reliable information. Consulting with a variety of teachers (e.g., classroom teacher, physical education instructor, art and music teachers) will increase the likelihood of gaining a complete picture of the student's behavior. Teachers may be asked to rate students in three areas: behavior, social skills, and academic performance. Some examples of behavior ratings are ADD-H Comprehensive Teacher's Rating Scale (ACTeRS; Ullmann, Sleator, & Sprague, 1985) shown in Form 3.9, School Situations Questionnaire-Revised (DuPaul & Barkley, 1990) shown in Form 3.10, the ADHD Rating Scale (DuPaul, 1990) shown in Form 3.11, and Attention Deficit Disorders Evaluation Scale, School Version (McCarney, 1989). Some examples of social skill ratings are Social Skill Rating System (Gresham & Elliot, 1990) and Walker-McConnell Scale of Social Competence and School Adjustment (Walker & McConnell, 1988). An example of academic performance scales is Academic Performance Rating Scale (DuPaul, Rapport, & Perriello, 1991).

Parent Interview

The interviewer will obtain the following information from the parent(s): frequency and severity of behavioral problems; health history, including prenatal, perinatal, and postnatal complications, the child's developmental history regarding the onset of the problem, and history of other significant medical disorders; possible correlation with other environmental factors (e.g., family disruptions); possible correlation with other psychological factors (e.g., anxiety, depression); parent-family psychiatric history; genetic factors (e.g., father also exhibiting signs of ADHD); parental management strategies and effectiveness; and a review of educational progress or placements.

Teacher Interview

The interviewer will obtain the following information from the teacher(s): frequency and severity of behavioral problem, the areas of difficulty for the student in both academic and social situations, the areas of success for the student in both academic and social situations, the most effective methods of instruction for the student, the current academic schedule of the student, the most effective methods of behavioral intervention for the student, and the level of interaction in social settings with peers and the development of peer relationships.

Student Interview

The interviewer will obtain the following information from the student: the student's perception regarding his or her behavior, the areas in which he or she has the most difficulty, the areas in which he or she is most successful, the student's methods of coping with the pressures associated with home and school activities, and the student's perceptions of how he or she gets along with peers in social situations. Although there are structured interview questions that are standardized, diagnosis should never be made solely on the basis of an interview with the student, even one using standardized questions.

Review of School Records

By examining all of a student's school records, the evaluator can obtain information concerning the following: the onset of difficulties in school, previous comments made by past teachers, the trend of success or failure in school, areas of strength and weakness, and the level of peer and social interaction. Use the School Developmental Summary (see Form 3.12) to collate and summarize the data.

Academic Classroom Performance Data

The evaluator should have access to current samples of the student's work to determine areas of strength and weakness, the ability of the student to organize his or her thoughts and put them in a final form, and the frequency of careless errors.

Psychoeducational Assessment

The administration of intelligence and achievement tests cannot directly evaluate the possibility of ADHD. The test results can only assist in identifying areas of strength and weakness. They may well, however, identify the possibility of coexisting areas of disability, such as a learning disability or a speech and language disorder. The psychoeducational assessment is often an optional component of the screening, included only as part of a full case study evaluation.

Medical Examination

The medical examination is crucial in ruling out any underlying medical factors that may be causing the student to exhibit symptoms of ADHD. This component is, however, the parents' decision and responsibility. If a medical diagnosis of ADHD has preceded the educational screening, the results of this diagnosis should be a part of the screening summary. In cases where ADHD has been diagnosed, the student may benefit from medication to assist him or her in sustaining attention and controlling impulsivity. Although there are no medical tests that can be used to confirm a diagnosis of ADHD, there are two tests that have been used solely for research purposes: magnetic resonance imaging (a scan depicting the brain's anatomy) and positron emission tomography (scans that measure the brain's metabolism). An EEG, which measures the brain's electrical activity, is given when evidence of epilepsy or other conditions exists. There are no blood or urine laboratory tests that can be used for the diagnosis of ADHD, although blood tests may well be used after medication has been prescribed and used.

Vision and Hearing Screening

Vision difficulties must always be eliminated at the outset as a possible cause for performance difficulties and inattention. A student who has a history of chronic ear infections frequently has a difficult time paying attention in class. Even though he or she may have passed the brief auditory screening at school, one cannot necessarily rule out hearing problems, particularly if the student has a history of frequent ear infections.

Step 5

When all screening components are completed, the results should be collated and documented on the Attentional Concerns Screening Results Form (Form 3.13). The team will then meet again, review the significance of the results, and make recommendations.

Step 5A

If the team determines that a comprehensive case study evaluation (CSE) is necessary, the usual procedures for initiating and completing a CSE will be followed.

Step 5B

A multidisciplinary conference (MDC) is held following the completion of the CSE and determination of eligibility is made. Note that a medical diagnosis of ADHD alone (without the multidisciplinary evaluation required by IDEA or the multisource data requirement of Section 504) does not *guarantee* eligibility under either P.L. 101-476 (IDEA) or Section 504. Many physicians are not aware of these requirements nor do they have access to the variety of data available in the school setting needed to do the multisource evaluation that is required. If results of the CSE indicate that the student is eligible for special education, the usual procedures are followed.

Step 6

If the team determines that a CSE is not warranted at this time, the MDC team will determine whether a 504 plan is needed. (See Form 3.14 for a Section 504 referral; Form 3.15 for the Parent-Guardian Consent for 504 Evaluation; Form 3.16 for the Notice of Conference; and Form 3.17 for the Section 504 Conference Summary). Care must always be taken in the Section 504 referral process to differentiate it from the special education referral process and to distinguish the types of services that will be available under Section 504 from the special education services that would have been provided should a student have been found eligible for special education services during the MDC. Uninformed parents and teachers with preconceived opinions about the outcome of the process can often create conflict and discord within the team if they have unreasonable expectations regarding special services or out-of-classroom placement for a student.

Another option at this time (if it has not previously been explored) may be a decision of the parents to obtain a medical evaluation (see Form 3.18 for a parental consent form to release school information to a physician). School staff should take care not to specifically *recommend* this option but rather, emphasize their willingness to cooperate by supplying information and carrying out educational interventions. A letter can be sent to the parents reminding them of the need for consent to release pertinent information (see Form 3.19). Once consent has been obtained, a follow-up letter should be sent to the parents encouraging them to make the doctor's findings available to school personnel (see Form 3.20). Under both Part B and Section 504, a team may determine that a student suspected of having ADHD is eligible for services without having received a medical evaluation or diagnosis. However, if a medical evaluation is required by the school district to determine eligibility, it is a related service that is to be provided at no cost to parents. The related service of medical evaluation required to determine eligibility is to be distinguished from ongoing medical service (e.g., treatment, follow-up), which is not a related service or school responsibility. A school district may take advantage of third-party funding, such as Medicaid or private insurance, to defray the cost of such evaluations. However, the use of private insurance must be with the parents' informed consent. Should a school district's use of third-party insurance deplete the parents' overall coverage or result in increased premiums, this would be a cost to the parents and would violate Part B-Section 504 requirements. The district would then be liable for reimbursing the parents for this cost.

Regardless of which option the building team recommends, the results of the attentional-concerns screening must be carefully interpreted. Because ADHD is difficult to diagnose and can often be confused with other disorders, care must be taken to remain focused on several key variables. In the school setting, the school psychologist will usually be responsible for compiling the test results and making preliminary recommendations, but the team will jointly reach a decision as to eligibility and treatment in the school setting. The following questions should be the focus during the discussion and decision-making process:

* What is the frequency of ADHD symptoms?
* What was the age of onset?
* At what frequency do the behaviors occur across a variety of settings?
* How do the symptoms interfere with the student's ability to function?
* What other factors might account for the ADHD-like symptoms?

Following a tentative diagnosis of ADHD by the building team (which should ideally be accompanied by the diagnosis of a health care professional), a comprehensive intervention plan must be developed that includes all aspects of a student's life—home, school, and extra-curricular activities.

Step 7

The assigned case manager will monitor interventions attempted at school. If the parents decide to pursue a medical evaluation, the case manager will be responsible for compiling the screening results as well as information about current interventions for the parents. The case manager will also complete the necessary forms to allow school personnel to communicate with the student's physician. The school nurse will be involved in and aware of any communication with the student's physician. If a 504 plan is written, a case manager will be assigned, and the plan will be reviewed yearly as per 504 guidelines.

WHAT ARE THE COMPONENTS OF A COMPREHENSIVE TREATMENT PLAN FOR ADHD?

The treatment of ADHD is both multifaceted and multidisciplinary and might well involve at least three other components in addition to educational services: medical therapy, family education, and counseling for parents or students or both. Chapter Four discusses the pros and cons of medication and includes suggestions and procedures for administering medication in the school setting. Chapter Five describes a wide variety of classroom interventions and strategies and suggests which district, school, and classroom practices provide the best environment for students with ADHD. Last, Chapter Six explains how you and your school staff can work with parents to help and advise them.

NOTES

1. *Jacobellis v. Ohio*, 378U.S. 184, 1964.

2. "ADD is a neurobiological disability. It is characterized by: attention skills that are developmentally inappropriate; impulsivity; and, in some cases, hyperactivity." (Memorandum, OCF, February 4, 1994).

3. Mary Fowler. "ADD Goes to School." *CH.A.D.D. Educators Manual: Attention Deficit Disorders*, pp. 11-16. Fairfax, VA: Caset Associates, 1988.

Attentional Concerns Flowchart

STEP 1: Parent, Teacher, Principal, Psychologist,
Social Worker, or Counselor Notes Attentional Concerns

STEP 2: Consultation Request Made to Building Level Team
(Building PPS/TAT Form Filled Out)
Vision and Hearing Screening Completed

STEP 3: Discuss Interventions Attempted/Additional
Interventions and Timelines

Determine Case Manager

Intervention Successful

More Intervention Needed

STEP 4: Secure Parent Permission
for Attentional Concerns Screening

Continue Interventions

STEP 5: Building Team Meets Again to Review Screening Results

No Case Study

STEP 5A: Case Study

STEP 6: Parent Conference

STEP 5B: Multidisciplinary
Staffing

Discuss Program Options

Not Eligible   Eligible

STEP 7: Determine Case Manager
and 504 Plan as Needed

Determine 504   Develop IEP
Eligibility

Set Review Date

Yearly Review   Yearly Review   Annual Review

Figure 3.1. Attentional Concerns Flowchart

NOTE: Adapted and reprinted by permission of West Chicago Elementary School District #33, West Chicago, IL. Readers may reproduce this document for their professional use.

FORM 3.1

TAT or PPS Sample Referral Form #1

BAILEY STREET ELEMENTARY SCHOOL
4561 Bailey Street
Canoga Park, CA 91303

Date _____

I. Student Identification

Name_____ Birth Date _____

Chronological Age_____

Parent's Name(s) _____

Address _____ Phone _____ (home) _____ (work)

Teacher _____ Grade _____

II. Review of Records and Past Educational History

Grade	School Attended	Program or Service*	Concerns
Pre-K			
K			
1			
2			
3			
4			
5			

*Could include ESL, bilingual, speech-language, Occupational Therapy or Physical Therapy consult, reading program, small group instruction, outside tutoring.

What services (if any) is the student presently receiving?

_____

III. Health Concerns

Student has missed _____ days this year.

Student missed _____ days last year.

Any health concerns? _____

Results: Vision screening _____ Date _____

          Hearing screening _____ Date _____

NOTE: Reprinted by permission of Currier Elementary School, West Chicago District #33, Chicago, IL. Readers may reproduce this document for their professional use.

IV. Academic Concerns

_____ Poor work completion in class
_____ Homework concerns
_____ Difficulty following written directions
_____ Difficulty following oral directions
_____ Poor retention of materials presented in class

Progress in the Following Subject Areas:

Math _____

Reading _____

Spelling _____

Written Work _____

(Creative expression as well as fine motor skills)

Academic Interventions

_____ One-on-one assistance provided (by whom?) _____
_____ Small group instruction
_____ Assignment book sent home
_____ Parent discussion about student's academic concerns
_____ Academic modifications and adaptations made
_____ Peer tutor assigned

Other Academic Strategies Used:

V. Behavioral Concerns

_____ Disruptive to other students _____ Lacks social skills
_____ Frequently off-task   _____ Disorganized
_____ Poor work attitude

Other Behavior Concerns:

Behavioral Interventions Attempted:

_____ Environmental changes made
_____ Discussion with parents
_____ Reinforcement program initiated
_____ Organizational program (e.g., check-in/check-out system for materials, homework)
_____ Classroom social skills training
_____ Consultation with building staff

FORM 3.2

TAT or PPS Sample Referral Form #2

BAILEY STREET ELEMENTARY SCHOOL
4561 Bailey Street
Canoga Park, CA 91303

Date _____

Student's Name _____ Grade _____ Birth date _____

Teachers _____

Check appropriate concerns and circle top two or three concerns:

_____ Disruptive	_____ Slow rate of work	_____ Overactive
_____ Poor attendance	_____ Cannot follow oral directions	_____ Inconsistent performance
_____ Off task	_____ Cannot follow written directions	_____ Poor peer relationships
_____ Disorganized (does not have appropriate supplies)	_____ Poor retention	_____ Works below grade level
_____ Doesn't complete assignments	_____ Poor study habits	_____ Health concerns
_____ Lacks initiative	_____ Poor attitude	_____ Distractible
_____ Lack of participation	_____ Speech or language functioning	

What modifications or adjustments have you made to remediate the problem? _____

_____

_____

What are the student's strengths?

_____

_____

_____

Have you involved the parents?   _____ Yes _____ No

NOTE: Reprinted by permission of West Chicago District #33, Chicago, IL. Readers may reproduce this document for their professional use.

Performance at Instructional Level

*Level   Teacher   Poor   Average   Above Average   Comments
(Indicate quality of work)*

Reading_____   _____

Mathematics _____

Language Arts_____

Social Studies _____

Science _____

Spelling_____

Related services student is receiving (e.g., speech or language,
counseling, Chapter I, bilingual)

_____

FORM 3.3

Sample Notification to Parents
of Attentional Concerns

BAILEY STREET ELEMENTARY SCHOOL
4561 Bailey Street
Canoga Park, CA 91303

Date _____

Dear ___(Parent or Guardian)__:

At a recent informational meeting on __(date)__ concerning your (son or daughter) __(name's)__ educational progress, the enclosed information was shared. [Include a summary of the discussion held at the informational meeting.] This information was also reviewed with you on __(date)__.

The enclosed information suggests that (name) is exhibiting the characteristics of a student with attentional difficulties. These difficulties, however, can only be diagnosed by a licensed physician. Should you decide to seek medical advice for your child in this regard, we would be glad to offer the physician any assistance he or she may need in making a diagnosis.

Please contact me if you have any questions regarding this matter. Thank you for your cooperation.

Sincerely,

_____
(Case Manager)

cc: Student File

FORM 3.4

Screening for Attentional Concerns—
Sample Parent Consent Form

A request for screening for attentional concerns was initiated by
___(School name)___ School's team on __(date)__. The screening results
will be used to better plan an educational program for your child.
Screening may include the following:

- Review of your child's school history
- Vision and hearing screening
- Classroom observation
- Parent and teacher rating forms
- Parent and teacher interview
- Student interview
- Home and school questionnaires

Please call _____(name)_____ at __(phone number)__ if you have any
questions.

* *

_____ I give my consent for the screening to be completed by school
personnel.

_____ I have concerns regarding the screening that I would like to
discuss further.

_____   _____
Date   Parent Signature

NOTE: Adapted and reprinted by permission of West Chicago Elementary District #33, West
Chicago, IL. Readers may use this document for their professional use.

FORM 3.5

Classroom Observation Record Protocol

Student _____   Observer _____

Age_____   Class Size and Type _____

Grade, Teacher _____   Time Started_____

Date _____   Time Stopped_____

School _____   Total Time _____

Reason for observation:

Classroom activity and explicit rules in effect at time of observation (attach copy of rules if applicable):

Description of observation techniques: (interval, time sample, length of interval)

Behavior Codes	*Grouping Codes*	*Teacher Reaction Codes*
T = on task	L = large group	AA = attention to all
V = off task, verbal	S = small group	A+ = positive attention to pupil
M = off task, motor	O = one-to-one	A– = negative attention to pupil
P = off task, passive	I = independent act	Ao = no attention to pupil
	F = free time	An = neutral attention to pupil

Time	*Pupil*	*Comparison Student*	*Class Scan*	*Anecdotal Notes*	*Teacher Reaction*
1.____	_____	_____	_____	_____	_____
2.____	_____	_____	_____	_____	_____
3.____	_____	_____	_____	_____	_____
4.____	_____	_____	_____	_____	_____
5.____	_____	_____	_____	_____	_____
6.____	_____	_____	_____	_____	_____
7.____	_____	_____	_____	_____	_____
8.____	_____	_____	_____	_____	_____

NOTE: Adapted and reprinted by permission of the author, Galen Alessi.

FORM 3.6

Behavior Observation Form

Child's Name: Date: Coder Initials:

Interval Number:	1	2	3	4	5	6	7	8	9	10	
Off task											
Fidgeting											
Vocalizing											
Playing with object											
Out of seat											
Interval Number:	11	12	13	14	15	16	17	18	19	20	
Off task											
Fidgeting											
Vocalizing											
Playing with object											
Out of seat											
Interval Number:	21	22	23	24	25	26	27	28	29	30	
Off task											
Fidgeting											
Vocalizing											
Playing with object											
Out of seat											
Interval Number:	31	32	33	34	35	36	37	38	39	40	Total
Off task											/40
Fidgeting											/40
Vocalizing											/40
Playing with object											/40
Out of seat											/40
										Total	/200

Comments:

NOTE: Adapted and reprinted by permission of West Chicago Elementary District #33, West Chicago, IL. Readers may reproduce this document for their professional use.

FORM 3.7

Home Situations Questionnaire

Child's Name_____ Date_____

Name of Person Completing This Form _____

Does this child present any behavior problems in any of these situations? If so, indicate how severe they are.

Situation	Yes No (Circle one)		If Yes, How severe? (Circle one) Mild Severe
While playing alone	Yes	No	1 2 3 4 5 6 7 8 9 10
While playing with other children	Yes	No	1 2 3 4 5 6 7 8 9 10
Mealtimes	Yes	No	1 2 3 4 5 6 7 8 9 10
Getting dressed	Yes	No	1 2 3 4 5 6 7 8 9 10
Washing-bathing	Yes	No	1 2 3 4 5 6 7 8 9 10
While you are on the telephone	Yes	No	1 2 3 4 5 6 7 8 9 10
While watching TV	Yes	No	1 2 3 4 5 6 7 8 9 10
When visitors are in your home	Yes	No	1 2 3 4 5 6 7 8 9 10
When you are visiting someone else	Yes	No	1 2 3 4 5 6 7 8 9 10
In supermarkets, stores, church, restaurants, or other public places	Yes	No	1 2 3 4 5 6 7 8 9 10
When asked to do chores at home	Yes	No	1 2 3 4 5 6 7 8 9 10
At bedtime	Yes	No	1 2 3 4 5 6 7 8 9 10
While in the car	Yes	No	1 2 3 4 5 6 7 8 9 10

FORM 3.8

ACTeRS Parent Form

Child's Name _____ Date _____

Teacher's Name _____

Below are descriptions of children's behavior. Please read each item and compare the statement with your child's behavior. Circle the numeral that most closely corresponds with your evaluation.

Behavior Item	Almost Never			Almost Always	
Attention Subscale	1	2	3	4	5
Works well independently (completes routine chores, homework, general hygiene without supervision or reminders).					
Hyperactivity Subscale	1	2	3	4	5
Overreacts (cries or becomes angry easily; extremely defensive, frustrates easily).					
Social Skills Subscale	1	2	3	4	5
Verbal communication clear and connected (able to tell a story from beginning to end without rambling or shifting topics).					
Oppositional Behavior Subscale	1	2	3	4	5
Starts fights over nothing (competitive and petty; frustrates easily and takes anger out on others).					
Early Childhood Scale	1	2	3	4	5
Difficult to comfort as a baby.					

FORM 3.9

ACTeRS (ADD-H Comprehensive Teacher's Rating Scale)

Child's Name_____ Date_____

Teacher's Name _____

Below are descriptions of children's behavior. Please read each item and compare the statement with your child's behavior. Circle the numeral that most closely corresponds with your evaluation.

Behavior Item	Almost Never			Almost Always	
Attention					
1. Works well independently	1	2	3	4	5
2. Persists with task for reasonable amount of time	1	2	3	4	5
Hyperactivity					
3. Extremely overactive (out of seat, on the go)	1	2	3	4	5
4. Fidgety (hands always busy)	1	2	3	4	5
Social Skills					
5. Behaves positively with peers-classmates	1	2	3	4	5
6. Verbal communication clear and "connected"	1	2	3	4	5
Oppositional					
7. Tries to get others into trouble	1	2	3	4	5
8. Starts fights over nothing	1	2	3	4	5

FORM 3.10

School Situations Questionnaire

Child's Name_____ Date_____

Name of Person Completing This Form _____

Does this child present any behavior problems for you in any of these situations? If so, indicate how severe they are.

Situation	Yes (Circle one)	No	If Yes, How severe? (Circle one)
			Mild Severe
While arriving at school	Yes	No	1 2 3 4 5 6 7 8 9
During individual desk work	Yes	No	1 2 3 4 5 6 7 8 9
During small group activities	Yes	No	1 2 3 4 5 6 7 8 9
During free-play time in class	Yes	No	1 2 3 4 5 6 7 8 9
During lectures to the class	Yes	No	1 2 3 4 5 6 7 8 9
At recess	Yes	No	1 2 3 4 5 6 7 8 9
At lunch	Yes	No	1 2 3 4 5 6 7 8 9
In the hallway	Yes	No	1 2 3 4 5 6 7 8 9
On field trips	Yes	No	1 2 3 4 5 6 7 8 9
During special assemblies	Yes	No	1 2 3 4 5 6 7 8 9
On the bus	Yes	No	1 2 3 4 5 6 7 8 9

FORM 3.11

ADHD Rating Scale

Child's Name _____ Age _____ Grade_____

Completed By _____

Rate each of the following items:	Not at All	Just a Little	Pretty Much	Very Much
1. Often fidgets or squirms in seat	0	1	2	3
2. Has difficulty remaining seated	0	1	2	3
3. Is easily distracted	0	1	2	3
4. Has difficulty awaiting turn in groups	0	1	2	3
5. Often blurts out answers to questions	0	1	2	3
6. Has difficulty following instructions	0	1	2	3
7. Has difficulty sustaining attention to tasks	0	1	2	3
8. Often shifts from one uncompleted activity to another	0	1	2	3
9. Has difficulty playing quietly	0	1	2	3
10. Often talks excessively	0	1	2	3
11. Often interrupts or intrudes on others	0	1	2	3
12. Often does not seem to listen	0	1	2	3
13. Often loses things necessary for tasks	0	1	2	3
14. Often engages in physically dangerous activities	0	1	2	3

NOTE: From the *ADHD Rating Scale: Normative Data, Reliability, and Validity* by George J. DuPaul, 1990, unpublished manuscript. University of Massachusetts Medical Center, Worcester, Massachusetts. Reprinted by permission of the copyright holder, George J. DuPaul, PhD. and does not extend to reproductions made from this publication.

FORM 3.12

School Developmental Summary

A. Identifying Information

Child's Name _____ Birth Date _____

Address _____ Telephone _____

School _____ Grade _____

B. Summary of Report Cards

	School Year	*Behavior Patterns*
Prekindergarten	_____	_____
Kindergarten	_____	_____
1st Grade	_____	_____
2nd Grade	_____	_____
3rd Grade	_____	_____
4th Grade	_____	_____
5th Grade	_____	_____
6th Grade	_____	_____
7th Grade	_____	_____
8th Grade	_____	_____

Summarized by: Name _____ Date _____

NOTE: Adapted and reprinted by permission of West Chicago Elementary District #33, West Chicago, IL. Readers may reproduce this document for their professional use.

FORM 3.13

Attentional Concerns Screening Results

Name_____

Address _____

School _____Grade _____ Date of Birth _____

Date of Meeting _____ Participants _____

_____

_____

School Development Summary completed (attach) Date _____

Vision screening results _____ Hearing screening results _____

Observation summary

Sample I   Activity type_____

        Date_____ Time_____

        Target % _____on-task behavior

        Completed by _____

Sample II   Activity type_____

        Date_____ Time _____

        Target % _____on-task behavior

        Peer % _____on-task behavior

        Completed by _____

Summary of observation:

_____

_____

_____

Parent rating form or interview (specify) _____

Results _____

Completed by _____ Date _____

_____

NOTE: Adapted and reprinted by permission of West Chicago Elementary District #33, West Chicago, IL. Readers may reproduce this document for their professional use.

Teacher rating form or interview (specify) _____

Results _____

Completed by_____ Date _____

Student interview

Results _____

Completed by_____ Date _____

Home and School Situations Questionnaires

Results _____

Completed by_____ Date _____

Summary, recommendations:

Follow up:

FORM 3.14

Sample Section 504 Referral

BAILEY STREET ELEMENTARY SCHOOL
4561 Bailey Street
Canoga Park, CA 91303

A. Personal Information:

Student _____ Birth Date _____

Parents _____ Phone _____

Address _____ Grade _____

Teacher _____ School_____

Referred by_____

B. Referral Information

1. Reason for referral:

    a. Condition:

    b. Major life activity affected:

    c. Description of the significant impacts:

2. Strategies or interventions initiated (attach copies of general education intervention documentation): ADHD Intervention Checklist*

_____   _____
Principal Signature   Date

_____   _____
Section 504 Coordinator Signature   Date

_____

NOTE: See Figure 5.1 in Chapter 5.
Adapted and reprinted by permission of West Chicago Elementary District #33, West Chicago, IL. Readers may reproduce this document for their professional use.

FORM 3.15

Sample Parent or Guardian Consent
for Section 504 Evaluation

BAILEY STREET ELEMENTARY SCHOOL
4561 Bailey Street
Canoga Park, CA 91303

(Date)_____

Dear: _____ (Parent-Guardian) _____

A referral for a 504 evaluation was made on (date) for your child,
_____ (child's name) _____ .

The evaluation is to determine if your child is eligible to receive 504 services that are provided by the public schools.

This evaluation is being requested because _____

_____

_____

Please check and sign below and return this form to your child's teacher. If you have further questions regarding the evaluation, please contact me at _(phone)_ .

Sincerely,

Building Principal

* *

Check one:

[ ] I give consent   [ ] I do not give consent.

_____   _____
Parent-Guardian Signature   Date

cc: Student's Cumulative File

_____

NOTE: Adapted and reprinted by permission of West Chicago Elementary School District #33, West Chicago, IL. Readers may reproduce this document for their professional use.

FORM 3.16

Notice of 504 Conference

BAILEY STREET ELEMENTARY SCHOOL
4561 Bailey Street
Canoga Park, CA 91303

To: _____ (Parent-Guardian) _____ Date: _____

Re: _____ (Student) _____

_____ To consider possible eligibility and provisions for services under Section 504 of the Rehabilitation Act of 1973.

_____ To review eligibility and services being provided for under Section 504 of the Rehabilitation Act of 1973.

_____ Other (specify)

Date of conference: Location and time of conference:

_____   _____

Conference participants (title, name)

Chairperson: _____

_____

_____

You have the right to bring other individuals, at your discretion, to this conference, including legal counsel. Please notify the district or program representative if you are in need of interpreting or translating services.

You also have the right to review your child's records and to request a hearing if you disagree with the district's identification, evaluation, provision of services, or change or termination of services under Section 504. If you desire a review of the records or wish to initiate a hearing, please contact:

_____   _____
(Name-Title)   (Phone)

_____

FORM 3.17

Section 504 Conference Summary

Student:_____ Date: _____

School: _____Grade: _____ Teacher: _____

Conference Participants: (Title, Name)

Chairperson: _____

_____

_____

Purpose of Conference:

_____ To consider eligibility and provision of services under Section 504

_____ To review eligibility and services provided under Section 504

_____ Other (Specify)

I. Identify Educational Concern:

II. Summary of Evaluation (if applicable):

Identify assessment procedure(s) and results:

III. Determination of Eligibility Under Section 504 (if applicable):

Consider and specify if a mental or physical condition significantly affects on one or more of the following activities: caring for oneself, performing manual tasks, walking, seeing, hearing, speaking, breathing, or learning *in the school setting*.

Condition	*Life Activity*	*Description of the Significant Impact In School Setting*

Check as appropriate:

_____ Student does *not* have a physical or mental impairment that substantially limits one or more major life activities, such as caring for ones self, performing manual tasks, walking, seeing, hearing, speaking, breathing, learning, and working.

NOTE: see Resource H. Adapted and reprinted by permission of West Chicago Elementary District #33, West Chicago, IL. Readers may reproduce this document for their professional use.

_____ Student has a physical or mental impairment that substantially limits one or more major life activities, such as caring for ones self, performing manual tasks, walking, seeing, hearing, speaking, breathing, learning, and working.

_____ Student does *not* need accommodation.

_____ Student does need accommodation (specify accommodation).

IV. General Education 504 Accommodation Plan

Describe the reasonable accommodations that are necessary:

V. Summary of Other Points of Discussion and Recommendations (if applicable):

VI. Targeted Date to Review the Service Plan (if necessary)

VII. Read carefully and sign below:

I have received a copy of the 504 Conference Summary and an explanation of the rights attached*

_____   _____
Signature of Parent-Guardian   (Date)

_____   _____
Signature of ADA/504 Coordinator   (Date)
or Committee chairperson

FORM 3.18

Authorization for Release or
Exchange of Confidential Information

Student: Name_____ Sex _____ Birth Date _____

Address: _____
                (include number, street, city, state, zip)

As the parent or legal guardian of the above-named child, I hereby grant
my permission to exchange information with: (List name and address)

_____

_____

Check those to be released:

_____ Student Permanent Record (basic identifying information;
          academic transcript; attendance records; health records;
          honors or awards; school-sponsored activities)

_____ Student Temporary Record (Family-background information;
          IQ scores; group & individual scores; psychological
          evaluations; achievement level test results; extra-curricular
          activities; disciplinary information)

_____ Special Education Records (Reports from multidisciplinary staffings
          on which placement was based; all records and reports relating
          to special education placement, hearings, and appeals)

_____ Occupational or Physical Therapy Evaluation Reports

_____ Psychological Evaluation Report or Diagnostic Test Scores
          (or both)

_____ Social and Health History

_____ Speech and Language Records and Reports

_____ Other

The purpose of this authorization is _____

_____   _____
Signature of Parent or Guardian   Date
                                                  Valid for one year

_____   _____
Signature of Student   Phone
(Age 12 and over)
                                             _____
                                             Person Securing Consent

NOTE: Adapted and reprinted by permission of West Chicago Elementary District #33, West
Chicago, IL. Readers may reproduce this document for their professional use.

FORM 3.19

Notification of Need
for Parental Consent

BAILEY STREET ELEMENTARY SCHOOL
4561 Bailey Street
Canoga Park, CA 91303

(Date)

Dear _(Parent or Guardian)_

As a follow-up to our recent discussion(s) regarding ___(child's name)'s attentional and/or academic difficulties, the educational staff at (school name) are willing to assist you in forwarding information to a physician.

At this point, we do not have a release signed to forward pertinent information. We would urge you to follow up with this most important matter in your child's education as soon as possible. Your contact person at (school name) will be (name and phone number) .

Please feel free to contact (him or her) so that we can be of further assistance.

Sincerely,

Case Manager

NOTE: Adapted and reprinted by permission of West Chicago Elementary School District #33, West Chicago, IL. Readers may reproduce this document for their professional use.

FORM 3.20

Notification of Release
of Confidential Information

BAILEY STREET ELEMENTARY SCHOOL
4561 Bailey Street
Canoga Park, CA 91303

(Date)_____

Dear (Parent or Guardian):

As a follow-up to our recent discussion(s) regarding   (child's name)   and his or her attentional-academic difficulties at school, information has been sent (with your written consent) to Dr.   (name)   on   (date) .

Please provide us with ongoing information regarding findings from Dr.   (name)   . This can be done by calling the contact person listed below, by sending notes to school, or by listing (contact person's name) at (school name) with your doctor to receive copies of reports. Your contact person at (school name) is (name) and the phone number is _____ .

Thank you for following up with this most important matter in your child's education.

Sincerely,

Case Manager

NOTE: Adapted and reprinted by permission of West Chicago Elementary District #33, West Chicago, IL. Readers may reproduce this document for their professional use.

4

THE MEDICATION OPTION

Is It the Answer?

When medication was recommended for my son [aged 10], I was very concerned, but after much research, I agreed to try it. The results were almost immediate. My son went from a second grade level to a fourth grade level in almost all of his subjects within a matter of time. My main concern is the long-term effects of the medication.

—Miriam Montgomery

I felt skeptical about the diagnosis of ADHD [in his sophomore year of high school]. It seemed like a scapegoat for what I thought was my laziness. But when I started taking medication, I could tell a dramatic difference in how I felt and how I thought.

—Matt Harris

Ritalin™ was prescribed though we would have preferred no medication. We decided to try it, but our son [aged 12] hated it. He said it made him feel weird and after a short time he refused to take it.

—Helen Brown

Medical therapy is the most controversial component of the treatment plan for ADHD, and although it has certainly proven helpful to many students, there are dangers in believing that drugs are the "magic bullet." Medication should only be prescribed and used after a thorough evaluation has been completed. This evaluation should take into consideration a child's behavior at home as well as at school. When a child is at risk of harming him or herself, when other non-medical interventions have proven insufficient, or when the child is at risk of significant failure, medication should be considered. But medication will not suddenly produce a child who gets all A's and never misbehaves. It can, however, often permit a child to attend to both learning and discipline in more productive ways. In spite of the positive results reported by many, there are those who are concerned about the increased use of the drug. The May 1996 issue of *AAP News*, a publication of the American Academy of Pediatrics, reports that the use of Ritalin™, the most commonly used drug prescribed for young people with ADHD, has increased from 3 tons in 1990 to over 8.5 tons in 1994; 90% of its use is in the United States.[1] The importance of combining other treatments (counseling, behavior modification, educational interventions, family therapy) cannot be overstated. Drugs alone are not the answer.

HOW CAN MEDICATION HELP?

Over 70% of children with ADHD who take medication exhibit behavioral, academic, and attentional improvements, according to parent-teacher ratings, laboratory task performance, direct observations, or a combination of these.[2]

There is a popular misconception that medications prescribed for ADHD act as tranquilizers on children. Nothing could be farther from the truth. These medications permit children (or at least about 75% of those studied) to function in a more normal fashion. Researchers and physicians are not absolutely certain about the way in which Ritalin™ works. It was once thought that Ritalin™ had exactly the opposite effect on children with ADHD than it did on children without ADHD. Hyperactive children would be calmed and nonhyperactive children would be stimulated. But researchers have since determined that stimulants work for non-ADHD individuals in exactly the same way they do for individuals with ADHD. Stimulants increase alertness and on-task behavior while decreasing impulsivity and distractibility in most adults and children, with or without ADHD. For the child with ADHD, the improvements can seem dramatic (when combined with other interventions). Improved attention and concentration, decreased distractibility, decreased activity level, and improved school performance can be some of the resulting behaviors.

IS RITALIN™ THE CURE?

Because ADHD is a syndrome and not a disease, there is no "cure." Medication alone will not be the answer to a student's symptoms of ADHD. ADHD is a chronic problem that the child will have throughout life. "You just don't write a prescription for medication without making changes in the child's school and home situation. Besides, without the right kind of support, the medication probably won't work."[3] The medications work best and are most helpful in an optimal environment. An optimal environment is one that is free from stress, inappropriate educational practices, poor nutrition, lack of structure and discipline, indulgent parenting, and few opportunities for achievement and building self-esteem. Dr. Theodore Mandelkorn compares using medication for ADHD to wearing glasses for a visual deficit. "Glasses do not make you behave, write a term paper, or even get up in the morning. They allow your eyes to function more normally, IF YOU CHOOSE to open them. YOU are still in charge of your vision."[4]

IS MEDICATION ABSOLUTELY NECESSARY?

Many parents manage the symptoms of ADHD without medication, particularly when the symptoms are not severe. Behavior modification, training, structure, and educational interventions are enough. But for many students, the problems are severe, and medication will be essential to see results with other interventions.

Many parents are reluctant to place their children on a medication that is still on the list of controlled substances for which the U.S. Drug Enforcement Administration sets annual production quotas. But recently, several medical groups, including the American Academy of Child and Adolescent Psychiatry and the national advocacy group, Children and Adults with Attention Deficit Disorders, filed a petition with the agency asking that Ritalin™ be removed from the controlled-substance list because it has not been found to be highly addictive, given the typical dosages prescribed.

WHAT MEDICATIONS ARE KNOWN
TO BE MOST HELPFUL?

Psychostimulants

The most commonly used medications are the psychostimulants: Ritalin™ (methylphenidate hydrochloride), Dexedrine™ (dextroamphetamine sulfate), and Cylert™ (magnesium pemoline). Note that the capitalized medication is a trademarked brand name, and the name following is the generic drug. These three psychostimulants are usually the first choice of physicians and are effective for attentional problems, impulsivity, and hyperactivity. Ritalin™ is most often prescribed for children 6 years of age and over, whereas in children 3 to 5, Dexedrine™ is more widely used. The psychostimulants offer positive effects on aggression and endurance in tasks. Ritalin™ has been used for over 50 years and is the most widely studied medicine given to children. It seldom results in serious side effects and has a well-documented history of results for boys, girls, and adolescents with childhood histories of ADHD. A short-acting medicine, the symptoms reappear when the dose wears off.

Ritalin™ is not recommended if the following conditions exist: high generalized anxiety, motor tics or a family history of Tourette syndrome, thought disturbances, parents or adolescent siblings who might abuse the drug (children do not), the child being under the age of 6 years, depression, agitation, hypertension, or glaucoma. Ritalin™ requires a written prescription from a physician every 30 days. The prescription cannot be called in over the phone to a pharmacy. An average cost for 1 month's supply of Ritalin™ can be as much as $70.00 depending on the strength and frequency of the dosage. Although the generic variety of methylphenidate hydrochloride is less expensive, it is not as effective as Ritalin™.

Dexedrine™ (dextroamphetamine sulfate) is the preferred stimulant for children under 6 years. It can be used with a child as young as 3 years old. If Ritalin™ has not proved effective with older children, Dexedrine™ is the preferred second choice. More than 70% of those children who take Dexedrine™ respond positively. Dexedrine™ is not recommended if the following conditions exist: cardiovascular disease, hypertension, hyperthyroidism, glaucoma, hypersensitivity, agitation, history of drug abuse, motor tics, or family history of Tourette syndrome. Dexedrine™ may seriously compound the effects of anxiety, bipolar disorder, thought disorders, hyperthyroidism, and hypertension and is not recommended when these conditions are present.

A third psychostimulant, Cylert™ (pemoline), builds up in the bloodstream and is taken only once per day. It is generally recommended after both Ritalin™ and Dexedrine™ have been tried unsuccessfully. Careful monitoring of the liver function is necessary, however, because this drug can affect the liver. Cylert™ is not recommended for a child with liver damage or disease, one whose family has a history of hepatic disorders, motor tics, history of Tourette syndrome, or seizure disorders. It can be used, however, with hypertension because it does not affect heart rate or blood pressure.

Antidepressants

The antidepressants constitute a second group of drugs that may be considered when psychostimulants do not work or create side effects such as tic disorders. This category of drugs includes Tofranil™ (imipramine hydrochloride), Norpramine™ (desipramine hydrochloride). Prozac™ (fluoxetine, and Wellbutrin™ (bupropion). Frequently finding the right dosage of drugs will take time.

Tofranil™, which is also used to treat enuresis is often used for children with ADHD who are anxious, have sleep problems, disturbed moods, a family history of depression or bipolar disorder, and those who have extreme anger and aggressiveness. This drug produces no rebound effect and must be given on weekends. Norpramine™ is not approved for children under 12 years. It is often used for those with anxiety amd depression symptoms that may coexist with ADHD.

Prozac™ is a newer drug that does not appear to be addictive or result in withdrawal symptoms. It is frequently used to treat anxiety, addictive disorders, bulimia, and excessive-compulsive disorders. This drug is very expensive, costing 20 times as much as some of the generic antidepressants.

When all other psychostimulants and antidepressants have not proven effective, Wellbutrin™ has been suggested for use. The research on the use of this medication is new, and much of it has not yet been published. Consult the pharmaceutical literature for suggested dosage and possible side effects.

Other Medications

The third group of medications is not really a group but a number of unique medications for very specific diagnosis: Tegretol™ (carbamazine), Catapres™ (clonide), Mellaril™ (thioridazine), Thorazine™ (chlorpromazine), and Haldol™ (haloperidol). Tegretol™, an anticonvulsant can be used for children ADHD who also have seizure disorders, especially complex partial seizures, which result in outbursts of aggressive behavior. Catapres™ is often used to treat high blood pressure in adults but has been shown to produce improvements in hyperactive and impulsive behavior while decreasing aggressive behavior and outbursts in children with ADHD. This drug is recommended for highly aroused, overactive children who respond poorly to stimulants or who have had persistent side effects from stimulants. It can also be used with children who have motor tics or Tourette Syndrome. One to two months of treatment time are needed to determine effectiveness, however. Antipsychotic drugs such as Mellaril™, Thorazine™, and Haldol™ are used to treat severe psychiatric disorders or children with severe anxiety that may mimic the symptoms of ADHD.

HOW DO THE MEDICATIONS WORK?

Medications for ADHD are believed to work in a similar fashion to insulin that is given to diabetics. In diabetics, the pancreas doesn't produce enough insulin, whereas in individuals with ADHD, their brains are not producing enough of the neurotransmitter chemicals, dopamine and norepinephrine. Ritalin™ and the other drugs used to treat ADHD are known to produce dopamine and norepinephrine, both of which increase blood flow in the areas of the brain controlling alertness and attention. With the brain's increased functioning comes an improved ability to attend, control impulses, become more cooperative, and be aware of social cues. Whereas the drug decreases the activity level of an ADHD child with hyperactivity, in ADHD children without hyperactivity, the drug increases alertness.

Contrary to the misinformation, rumors, and innuendo that circulated in the press a number of years ago, the psychostimulants do not change a child's basic personality or values. They do not exert some sinister control over a child's mind; the child has total freedom to choose how he or she wants to behave. By taking the drugs, students with ADHD can successfully choose to exercise self-control, pay attention to tasks, be persistent and thoughtful, and function more normally in school and at home. Researchers report improved peer relations, student-teacher relations, and family interactions as a result of medication. Even sports, music, and other nonacademic activities are positively affected. Using stimulants does not lead to aggressive, assaultive, or addictive behavior. Research has also shown that using stimulants does not lead to a greater risk of substance abuse in later life.

WHAT ARE THE SIDE EFFECTS?

No major side effects are reported for Ritalin™, in use since the early 1950s, or Dexedrine™, in use even longer, nor is there correlation between reliance on these drugs and later drug abuse. Any medication, whether by prescription or over-the-counter, must be used with discretion and in accordance with doctor's orders, warning labels, and common sense.

Short-term side effects that occur frequently but are not usually severe are (a) appetite disturbances (not being hungry, some mild sense of stomach upset, or both); (b) sleep disturbances, such as insomnia; (c) rebound hyperactivity; and (d) increased irritability or mood change. Of more concern to parents are reported long-term effects. At one time, decreased growth was thought to be a problem for children who took Ritalin™. However, research has not substantiated any significant differences in growth curves between children on or off the medication when followed through adolescence. Nevertheless, most physicians monitor height and weight as well as obtaining an annual complete blood count and chemical profile. Stimulants are of course discontinued if any problems are noted. Of more serious concern is the occurrence of motor tics (muscle twitches or abnormal motor movements). Any nervous tic that occurs in association with Ritalin™ should be reported to a doctor immediately.

Among the most common side effects of antidepressants like Torfranil™ and Norpramine™ in children are nervousness, sleep disturbances, fatigue, or mild gastrointestinal upsets. These problems are usually short term in nature and can often be eliminated by reducing the dosage.

Frequently reported as side effects for both pyschostimulants and antidepressants are lethargy, depression, or becoming a "glassy-eyed zombie." Rather than being side effects of the medication, these are indications that the dosage of the medication is too high, the child is on the wrong medication, or that the diagnosis is incorrect.

HOW IS THE CORRECT
DOSAGE DETERMINED?

Physicians consider two variables when determining the correct dosage for an individual—body size and the severity of the symptoms. If Ritalin™ (or another psychostimulant) has been prescribed, the child will often begin at a dosage of one pill (5 mg.) twice a day, approximately 4 hours apart, usually in the morning and before lunch. By taking the pill before lunch, the dosage will be effective by the time a child returns to the classroom after lunch. The doctor will ask parents and teachers to watch carefully for behavior changes, and if none are noted, the dosage can be raised 2.5 to 5 mg. per dose every 3 or 4 days until gradual improvement is noted. If side effects are noticed, the dosage will have to be moderated. Younger children may start with a smaller dosage and have it raised more gradually. Those children with severe rebound hyperactivity may need a third dosage. Some doctors will administer a stimulant medication trial. Others feel there is no need for a placebo versus a drug trial because the changes in behavior observed when children take psychostimulants are so dramatic. Some physicians prefer that neither the teacher nor the child know when they are taking the drug and when they are taking the placebo so that the behavior monitoring will be completely objective.

Now available are time-released versions of the short-acting stimulants, Ritalin™ and Dexedrine™: Ritalin SR™ and Dexedrine Spansule™. They have the advantage of lasting up to 8 hours rather than just 2 to 3 hours. Having to take only one pill is a big advantage for children who are forgetful or who are embarrassed to be seen taking medication in front of their friends. The time-release forms do, however, have their disadvantages. The medication takes much longer to reach its peak effect and sometimes never achieves as strong an effect as the child needs at critical times.

HOW CAN MEDICATIONS BE SAFELY
ADMINISTERED AT SCHOOL?

Consult your school board policies for the regulations and procedures that cover the administration of medication in your district. Table 4.1 illustrates a sample board policy covering the administration of medicines to students. Form 4.1 contains a school medication authorization form to be completed by the parent and the child's physician. Here are some helpful strategies for making sure your students take their medication on time:

- Assign staff member (e.g., secretary, health aide) to remind student to take medication.
- Provide teacher with student's medication schedule.
- Provide positive verbal praise.
- Have the school nurse educate the student on the benefits of taking a particular medication.
- Have an adult or peer escort the student to the office for medication.
- Have the student wear a digital watch with an alarm as a reminder.
- Use a school-home reward system for complying with medication.

HOW CAN TEACHERS HELP PHYSICIANS MONITOR THE USE OF MEDICATION?

Determining the dosage and medication that will best meet the needs of a student can often be a laborious and time-consuming process for everyone concerned. Teachers may be asked to assist the physician in evaluating behavioral changes in responses to differing dosages or medications. One quick and easy way to do this is to choose a task that is done each day or week and requires attention and freedom from distraction. Examples include weekly spelling tests, daily handwriting assignments, or practice math problems. By observing the same activity each time, the teacher will be able to offer a more objective viewpoint. Teachers may also be asked to offer a more exhaustive follow-up evaluation (see Form 4.2).

WHAT ABOUT ALTERNATIVE TREATMENTS?

Some parents put off using medication because they want to try alternative treatments first. Yet many of these are either unproven or proven to be ineffective. Here are some of the more common alternative therapies:

Special Diets

The Feingold Diet has been around for over 20 years, and although many extravagant claims have been made regarding its effectiveness in improving activity level, behavior, school work, and even physical symptoms such as muscle pains and headaches, the evidence is nonexistent. The menu eliminates additives from the diet. "In the past fifteen years, dozens of well-controlled studies published in peer-reviewed journals have consistently failed to find support for Dr. Feingold's approach."[6]

Megavitamin Therapy

During the past decades, interest in megadosing children with vitamins (orthomolecular therapy) gained some popularity. Large amounts of niacin, ascorbic acid, pyridoxine, and calcium were purported to cause improvements in children with learning and attention disabilities. Although vitamin supplements are often recommended by pediatricians, there is no supporting evidence for megavitamin therapy. Some of the vitamins recommended for the megavitamin therapy can have toxic effects when given over long periods of time in large doses. There is a risk for young children, whose liver functions might not be able to break down and eliminate such substances from their bodies. Niacin can cause flushing, itching, decreased blood pressure, and excessive sleepiness as well.

Sensory Integration Training

This treatment was developed out of the field of occupational therapy by Dr. Jean Ayres, an occupational therapist based in California. Treatment involves working with a physical therapist to practice exercises believed to be important in developing better visual-motor coordination. Dr. Ayres hypothesized that the vestibular system (organ of balance in the inner ear) played a critical role in learning disabilities and attention disorders. Scientific studies have found little or no benefit from these exercises, and although they are natural and certainly not harmful, they are not recommended for the treatment of ADHD.

Play Therapy

This type of therapy is really intended for children who have suffered severe emotional distress growing out of trauma or dysfunctional parenting. Unless there is a serious, documented emotional disorder coexisting with the ADHD, there is no valid reason for treating ADHD with play therapy.

Chiropractic Treatment

Based on the idea that brain tissue was lodged or pinched between the bony plates of the skull, chiropractic treatment put forceful pressure on these plates, ostensibly to release the tissues and tension. This treatment has no scientific basis and may in fact be painful if not harmful.

Anti–Motion Sickness Medication

The proponents of this theory have hypothesized a relationship between ADHD and problems of coordination and balance. They recommend a treatment of anti–motion sickness medication along with vitamins. There are no scientific studies to support this theory.

Osteopathic Treatment

Osteopaths assume that the things that go wrong with the human body are the result of pressure of displaced bones on nerves and are curable by physical manipulation. Although osteopaths concur with current thinking when they claim that children with learning and attention problems have documented difficulties that are related to the central nervous system's functioning, they erroneously link these problems to malfunctions in the musculoskeletal system. Current research indicates that ADHD has its origins in the malfunctioning of neurotransmitters in the brain rather than abnormalities within the central nervous system itself.

Candida Yeast Treatment

Candida albicans is a yeast that grows in the human body. Infections of the vagina, mouth, skin, and nails can result when this yeast overpowers the immune system and gets out of control. Some have hypothesized that the weakened immune system is then susceptible to many illnesses, including ADHD. The theory is not consistent with what is known about the cause of ADHD and has not been investigated in a rigorous, scientific manner.

Irlen Lenses

Psychologist Helen Irlen has hypothesized that learning disabilities and attention disorders are caused by a neurological condition labeled *scotopic sensitivity syndrome* (SSS). This condition causes perceptual problems related to light source, light intensity, wave length, and color contrast.[6] She claims that 50% of individuals who are reading disabled actually suffer from SSS and can be helped with specially tinted lenses know as Irlen lenses or Irlen filters. Although there is no evidence to support her theory or the effectiveness of her treatment, glowing testimonials from satisfied customers keep her theory alive.

OcularMotor Training

This proposal for treating not only ADHD but also reading disorders and learning disabilities with eye exercises has no research to support its effectiveness. The eye movement exercises proposed by some optometrists were thought to overcome patterns of abnormal eye movements in children with these disorders. The group of optometrists who offer treatment in ocularmotor training are called behavioral optometrists, and they target specific skills in their training program, such as tracking, fixation, binocularity, and focus change. ADHD does not arise out of problems with the eye muscles or their movements. In 1984, the American Academy of Pediatrics, in conjunction with the American Association for Pediatric Ophthalmology and Strabismus and the American Academy of Ophthalmology, issued a policy statement that included these conclusions:

> There is no peripheral eye defect that produces dyslexia and associated learning disabilities. Eye defects do not cause reversal of letters, words or numbers. . . . [N]o known scientific evidence supports the claims for improving the academic abilities of dyslexic or learning-disabled children with treatment based on visual training, including muscle exercises, ocular pursuit or tracking exercises, or glasses (with or without bifocals or prisms).[8]

Biofeedback

Biofeedback combines the use of relaxation exercises with electronic monitoring of muscle tension, which is then fed back to the person through displays of light on a panel or TV monitor or through different pitches of tones. This treatment is believed to relax muscle tension in various muscle groups of the body, thereby creating a calming effect on hyperactivity.

A variation of this treatment, EEG feedback or neurofeedback, was developed by Dr. Joel Lubar of the University of Tennessee. The finding that children with ADHD seem to have less brain electrical activity, especially in the frontal lobes of the brain, encouraged Dr. Lubar to believe that if this electrical activity could be measured and converted to a color or sound monitor of some type, children with ADHD could be taught ways to monitor and increase this electrical activity. Although the proponents make grandiose claims for the treatments, in studies using double-blind controls, the evidence is nonexistent as to its effectiveness in improving the symptoms of ADHD. The cost of these treatments is substantial ($3,000 to $6,000), and the trappings are impressive (equipment, wires, treatment rooms), so reports of success may be tied to the kind of expense and effort that parents have expended to participate. The treatment is certainly not a proven, nonpharmacological treatment for ADHD, as advertised.

When parents come to you asking for advice regarding any of these methodologies, be cautious in your condemnation of them. Do, however, encourage parents to do more reading and research before they spend vast sums of money or enroll in complex training programs. Suggest that parents keep in mind the following questions suggested by Ingersoll:[9]

1. Is this theory consistent with existing knowledge in related fields such as anatomy, medicine, psychiatry, psychology, and education?
2. Is the theory consistent with what is specifically known about ADHD and learning disabilities?
3. What is the quality of the scientific evidence that indicates that the treatment is effective?
4. What are the costs involved, and what, if any, are the dangers associated with this treatment?

▰▰▰▰▰▰▰

NOTES

1. Luann Zanzola. May 1996, Medical Experts Defend Against Ritalin Charges. *AAP News*, p. 10.

2. Russell A. Barkley. (1988). A Review of Stimulant Drug Research with Hyperactive Children. *Journal of Child Psychology and Psychiatry, 18,* 137-165.

3. Bennett Shaywitz as quoted in Mary Fowler. *Maybe You Know My Kid: A Parent's Guide to Identifying, Understanding, and Helping Your Child with Attention-Deficit Hyperactivity Disorder.* Secaucus, New Jersey: Birch Lane Press, 1990, p. 108.

4. Theodore D. Mandelkorn. "Thoughts on the Medical Treatment of ADHD." *The CH.A.D.D.ER Box,* May 1993, 6(3), p. 1.

5. For a more detailed discussion of medications, their side effects and benefits, see Copeland, Edna D. *Medications for Attention Disorders and Related Medical Problems.* Atlanta, GA: Resurgens Press, Inc., 1994.

6. Sam Goldstein and Barbara Ingersoll. "Controversial Treatments for Children with Attention Deficit Hyperactivity Disorder." In Children and Adults with Attention Deficit Disorder (CH.A.D.D.), *Educators Manual: Attention Deficit Disorders,* pp. 77-78. Fairfax, VA: Caset Associates, 1992.

7. Barbara Ingersoll, *Your Hyperactive Child: A Parent's Guide to Coping with Attention Deficit Disorder.* New York: Doubleday, 1988, p. 202.

8. Ibid., p. 198.

9. Ibid., p. 86.

TABLE 4.1 Sample School Board Policy Regarding Student Welfare: Administering Medicines to Students

The Board of Education recognizes that the administration of medication to students during the school day may be necessary.

The Board of Education further recognizes that there are certain state and federal laws that govern the administration of medication to students in certain circumstances.

Parent(s) or guardian(s) have the primary responsibility for administering medication to their children. Administering medication during school hours or during school-related activities is discouraged unless it is necessary for the critical health and well-being of the student. Teachers and other nonadministrative school employees, except certified school nurses, shall not be required to administer medication to students. Parent(s) or guardian(s) may authorize their child to self-administer a medication according to the District's procedures for student self-administration of medication.

Nothing in this policy shall prohibit any school employee from providing emergency assistance to students, including the administration of medication.

Wherefore the school administration is hereby directed to promulgate regulations and guidelines as are necessary to comply with laws and regulations.

NOTE: Reprinted by permission of West Chicago Elementary District #33, West Chicago, IL. Readers may reproduce this document for their professional use.

FORM 4.1

School Medication
Authorization Form

Student's Name: _____

Address: _____

Telephone Number: _____

Birth Date: _____

School: _____

Grade: _____

Emergency Telephone Number: _____

I ___(name),___ parent or guardian of ___(child's name),___ hereby authorize XYZ School District and its employees and agents, on my behalf and stead, to administer to my child, (or to allow my child to self-administer, while under the supervision of the employees and agents of the School District,) lawfully prescribed medication in the manner described below. I further acknowledge and agree that, when the lawfully prescribed medication is so administered, I waive any claims I have against the School District or its employees and agents arising out of the administration of said medication. In addition, I agree to indemnify and hold harmless the School District, its employees and agents, as a group or individually, from and against any and all claims, damages, causes of action, or injuries, including reasonable attorney's fees and costs expended in defense thereof, incurred or resulting from the administration of said medication.

Parent or Guardian Signature _____ Date _____

To be completed by the student's physician:

Name of medication _____

Dosage:_____ Time:_____

Type of disease or illness:_____

Must this medication be administered during the school day to allow the child to attend school?   Yes   No
_____

Are there any side effects to the medication?   Yes   No

If yes, please specify:_____

Can this child self-administer medication
on field trips?   Yes   No

Doctor's Name (please print)   Doctor's Signature

_____   _____

Address _____

Telephone Number _____

Emergency Telephone Number _____

<u>**FORM 4.2**</u>

ADD Medication Follow-Up Report

Student _____ Date _____

Parent or Guardian _____

Teacher _____ School Counselor _____

Physician _____

Current medication _____ Dosage _____

Time administered at school _____

Observations:

Have you noticed or has the student complained of any of the following side effects?

How Often and When?

_____ Decreased appetite _____

_____ Insomnia _____

_____ Stomachaches _____

_____ Headaches _____

_____ Prone to crying _____

_____ Tics or nervous movements _____

_____ Dizziness _____

_____ Drowsiness _____

_____ Anxiety _____

_____ Social withdrawal _____

_____ Irritability _____

_____ Sadness _____

_____ Staring _____

Have you noticed any fluctuations in behavior throughout the day?
If so, describe.
_____

NOTE: Permission to reprint (or adapt) this material is granted by the Kenosha Unified School District No. 1/Division of Special Services, Kenosha, WI. Readers may reproduce this document for their professional use.

Describe the student's attentiveness (i.e., distractibility, listening, on-task behavior, concentration).

Describe the student's impulse control (i.e., acting before thinking, shifting from one activity to another, supervision required, interrupting, awaiting turn).

Describe the student's physical activity level (i.e., ability to sit still or remain seated, always on the go).

Current Academic Levels:

_____ Excellent _____ Good _____ Fair _____ Poor

Current Peer Interactions:

_____ Excellent _____ Good _____ Fair _____ Poor

Other Concerns:

cc: Physician
Parent
Student's Cumulative File

5

DESIGNING A PROGRAM TO MAXIMIZE EACH STUDENT'S POTENTIAL

Policies, Practices, Interventions, and Strategies That Work

The best teachers have creative energy, confidence, and are not confrontational or highly authoritarian in personality. They also have a deep sense of working as a team with the parents and the support staff for the child's best interests.

—Karen Beacon

When I met with Daniel's kindergarten teacher the first time to tell her that he had ADHD and offer my assistance with developing a reward system for him, here's what she had to say: " Too many kids are diagnosed with ADD and the problems are just due to immaturity. He needs to learn to mind. I don't believe in rewarding behavior that is expected."

—Shelley Burns

The kids pick on me. People tell on me because I think out loud and I start singing or tapping my feet. Heather always says, "Brett, be quiet!" I get embarrassed when I get in trouble.

—Brett Adams

Nowhere do the symptoms of ADHD affect a child's life so dramatically as in the school environment. Even if the symptoms of ADHD have gone unnoticed at home, a child's enrollment in kindergarten will probably signal the end of peaceful oblivion regarding the disorder (particularly for those children with a high degree of hyperactivity and impulsivity). About a third of the children with ADHD have problems achieving at the level predicted by their IQ scores. One has only to read comments on the report cards of students with ADHD and the sad tale is told. "Mary isn't working up to her potential." "I know that Sam could do better if only he tried harder." "Sally is very bright, but she isn't turning in her homework." And these are the students who, without the disability of ADHD, would be honor roll material but are currently making C's and D's. An even larger percentage of students with ADHD (between 30% and 70%) have failed at least 1 year of school and are at risk for dropping out. The picture is not a pretty one. But there is hope. The pages ahead contain strategies, interventions, and suggestions for how you and your teachers can work with students who have ADHD to maximize their potential.

WHAT KINDS OF PROBLEMS DO STUDENTS WITH ADHD HAVE?

The catalog of problems that students with ADHD have in school makes for very depressing reading. These eager cherubs come bouncing (sometimes literally off the walls) into kindergarten at the age of 5 or 6 and immediately, their excessive activity and vocalization put the teacher on notice that here is a child who won't be ignored for long. They can't sit still during story time; they grab toys during playtime; they push and shove when they're waiting in line for drinks or the bathroom; and they may throw a temper tantrum or two just to show the teacher who's in charge. Their enthusiasm for any task lasts only as long as it takes the teacher to look in another direction, and their cubbies soon resemble giant garbage heaps of school newsletters that never made it home, forgotten belongings, and broken crayons. They interrupt when the teacher is giving instructions and want to talk about irrelevant topics when the class is learning about seashells. Their classmates soon shun them, and before the year is ended, their enthusiasm for school has turned sour. Their parents are devastated; the teacher is frustrated; and the poor child is launched on a downward spiral of "bad feelings." "I'm no good," "I'm dumb," and "Nobody likes me," are frequently repeated phrases from the lips of early elementary children with ADHD.

The problems will compound as the child gets older. Lowered self esteem and frustration at not being able to measure up to the expectations of parents and teachers will create behavior problems and possibly even depression. That's the bad news. The good news is that more and more is being discovered about how to create schools and classrooms that are conducive to meeting the needs of students with ADHD. Teachers and specialists are receiving training and consequently developing a greater degree of empathy and understanding for their young charges. There has never been a more hopeful time, in my opinion, for children with ADHD in schools.

WHAT DOES THE RESEARCH SAY?

Researchers are only recently beginning to investigate promising intervention and identification practices for students with ADHD. But the early findings come as no surprise to those of us who have long been students of the effective-schools literature. Here are some of the factors that positively influence the educational outcomes of students with ADHD:

- Attention to individual student differences when designing specific educational plans
- A common commitment on the part of personnel
- Inservice training for professionals who work with students who have ADHD
- Development of an appropriate match between teacher expectations and student performance
- Recognition of the importance of social competencies, and training to develop them
- Strong fiscal and staff support for the development and implementation of promising practices
- Genuine commitment to working with students' families[1]
- Academic instruction that combines inclusion of the student with ADHD in the majority of regular classroom instruction
- Behavior management that includes a well developed plan to help the child learn how to manage his or her own behavior in the classroom

- Classroom accommodations or changes that recognize the special needs of the child with ADHD[2]

WHAT KIND OF SCHOOL IS BEST FOR STUDENTS WITH ADHD?

As an elementary school principal, my staff and I determined that if our school had the following five characteristics, *any* child's chances of academic success would increase. I believe these same characteristics are even more crucial to success for those students with ADHD. Here they are: (a) a learning success philosophy, (b) clear rules and expectations, (c) consistent implementation of consequences, (d) structure and organization, and (e) rich motivational programs with incentives. If all of these beliefs and behaviors do not pervade the school and are not practiced by all of the staff members (including secretaries, custodians, classroom aides, and lunchroom supervisors, etc.), the "success for all" philosophy is diminished. Here are the five characteristics explained in more detail:

*The administration and staff members
believe that all students can learn.*

I was an elementary school principal for 8 years. The motto of our school was, "All can learn." These words were painted in a prominent place in the school hallway where every student and teacher saw them each day. The philosophy that all students can learn means that not only are expectations high but that teachers do whatever it takes to bring a child to mastery of important skills and concepts. Whether it takes more time, different materials, or another instructional approach, the teacher (and his or her support team) have a responsibility to find a way.

*The rules and expectations for behavior
in the school are clearly stated and
consistently applied in all classrooms
and learning areas.*

There is nothing more confusing for a child than to master one set of rules in his or her classroom and then find out that the librarian or gym teacher operates from a totally different set of rules. When a staff can reach consensus on the core rules that must be followed by all students regardless of the setting and can clearly state these for members of the school family, students with ADHD are much more likely to follow those rules. Our faculty spent time discussing and deciding what rules were basic to the smooth running of our school and then had signs professionally printed for every classroom and hallway. If a student (or faculty member) had a problem remembering the rule, it was clearly visible for all to see.

> *Consequences for breaking the rules are swiftly*
> *and fairly administered to all students,*
> *but especially so for students with ADHD.*

Discipline must be attended to with consistency, firmness, fairness, and expediency. There must be an organized system for dispensing consequences, and this system must work like clockwork. Every staff member must know his or her role and play it well. Administrative backup and encouragement are crucial. Parental support in structuring consequences is very important. Creativity and flexibility are essential.

> *The school is well-ordered and structured.*

All staff members must be proactive. They must anticipate possible problems and plan for contingencies. Field trips, assemblies, holiday programs, substitute teachers, classroom parties, fire drills, and special events (e.g., balloon launch, a visit from the zoo keeper with live specimens, or a drama presentation by a local play group) are fraught with the possibility of upset for the child with ADHD. During these times, the order, structure, constancy, and predictability of routines can help, and so can an early warning system that lets a child know what is coming.

> *The school staff believes in positive reinforcement,*
> *incentive programs and motivational activities.*

Students with ADHD need much more positive reinforcement from teachers and other staff members than students without ADHD. If staff members take the position that it's the responsibility of students to learn and if they don't, "it's not my problem," the culture of the school will not be supportive of changing some of the traditional approaches that may stand in the way of school success for all. Motivational and incentive programs need to change constantly, and what worked last month may be "old hat" by next month. Staff members must be willing to explore enough options to find out what works with a given student.

WHAT TYPES OF PRINCIPALS ARE MOST EFFECTIVE?

Here are the top 10 characteristics of principals who are most effective for all students (but especially those with ADHD):

1. Runs a tight ship with regard to discipline, structure, and organization
2. Knows how to procure resources for materials, programs, and inservice training
3. Attends TAT-PPS meetings and staffings regularly, and participates collaboratively in all decisions involving student placement
4. Listens to parents and their concerns
5. Visits classrooms regularly, and is aware of the needs of teachers
6. Thinks and solves problems creatively by coming up with one more plan, one more idea, or one more solution
7. Holds both teachers and students to high expectations
8. Believes that all can learn (this includes both teachers and students)
9. Spends time with students (in the lunchroom, on the playground, and in the classroom)
10. Affirms, supports and encourages teachers[3]

WHO ARE THE BEST TEACHERS?

All the teachers in your school should be educated, flexible, intelligent, cooperative, open-minded, structured, confident, knowledgeable, and well-trained. But if they aren't, the students without ADHD can usually manage to compensate for a year with less than the best. The situation isn't ideal, but "average" students have more coping strategies, higher self-esteem, more intrinsic motivation, and adequate rule-governed behavior. Capable learners pick up memorization and organizational strategies on their own, almost by osmosis, it seems. The child with ADHD, on the other hand, can't survive without direct instruction in these "helpful hints." A child with ADHD needs the best every day, from the starting bell until dismissal time. A child with ADHD can scarcely cope with his or her own skill deficiencies. How can he or she be expected to compensate for a teacher's lack of skill?

Observing an effective classroom teacher at work is like watching a conductor directing a symphony orchestra. The process looks effortless until you know the exceptional skill it involves. What kinds of qualities does the effective teacher possess that are so important to the academic success of a child with ADHD? The effective teacher is all of these:

* Informed and educated about the symptoms of and the treatments for ADHD
* Empathetic about the struggles of a child with ADHD
* Loving, kind, and supportive
* Highly structured and organized
* Calm and nonreactive
* Willing to recognize, reward, and encourage positive behavior
* Articulate about expectations
* Flexible and willing to change
* Communicative and empathetic with parents
* Able to teach a concept using many different approaches
* Tenacious about student learning and success

HOW DO THESE TEACHERS RESPOND TO STUDENTS WITH ADHD?

Teaching is a stressful and demanding responsibility, requiring excellent emotional, psychological, and physical health from its professionals, as well as outstanding instructional methods. Teachers who can effectively meet the needs of students with ADHD must be peak performers.

Taylor has identified six key areas in which every teacher who works with ADHD students must excel.[4] This paragon of virtue must be able to do these things:

Guard a Student's Self-Esteem

A student's self-esteem is very fragile, and a skilled teacher will do everything in his or her power to protect it and build it up. Brett Adams had a temporary setback when he transferred to a new school in third grade and encountered a teacher who temporarily shattered his self-esteem. The teacher screamed at Brett in front of the class and a visiting parent, telling him that if he couldn't sit down and shut up, she didn't want to see him at school on Monday. Needless to say he wasn't there. Now in another setting, he's thriving. His current teacher is understanding of his needs, and his mother reports that "everyone seems to really love Brett, even though he can be difficult."

Build Up a Student's Strengths

Critical to a student's success in school is the identification of those things he or she does well. The skilled teacher will help to find those strengths and then affirm and encourage a student so that he or she feels special.

Pace a Student's Work

Students with ADHD demonstrate what is known as a *production deficit* when they encounter the demands of written work in the classroom. Students with ADHD do not have the motivation and persistence that keeps others churning through mountains of seat work, and the student with ADHD will be buried under piles of homework unless a sensitive teacher decreases the workload to accommodate the child's handicapping attentional deficit. This can be accomplished by carefully monitoring assignments and determining more accurately when a concept or skill has been mastered. If reducing the workload isn't possible, then breaking up the assignment into smaller parts will serve the same purpose. Skilled teachers will weigh the issue of accuracy versus productivity and work on the latter before addressing the former.

Modify the Grading System

The skilled teacher is able to answer the question, "What is the purpose of schooling?" and having answered that question correctly ("to help students learn how to study and learn"), will judiciously modify his or her grading systems to avoid destroying the self-esteem and self-confidence of a child with ADHD.

Help a Student Socially

The other students in the ADHD child's classroom will take their cues on how to react and treat that child from the adult role model in that classroom, the teacher. If he or she includes the child in the group; prevents and takes a proactive approach to behavior rather than a punitive, reactive approach; and uses humane and sensible disciplinary methods, the student will have the ideal social setting in which to grow and mature.

Use Effective Educational Methods

This is the last and the most important assignment of the classroom teacher—teaching critical skills and concepts to students on a daily basis. Does the teacher have a clear idea of the outcomes for his or her grade level? Is he or she skilled at modifying curriculum and presenting material to meet the needs of different learning styles? Is the classroom well-organized and structured? Teachers at the elementary school level traditionally have received more training and been more willing to "teach the child" rather than "teaching the subject." But many high school faculties are in the forefront of adaptations for students with ADHD. The Michigan Department of Education has developed an excellent set of strategies and techniques to enhance middle school and high school instruction for students with ADHD. These can be found in Appendix G.

HOW DO THE BEST TEACHERS TEACH?

The following 18-item checklist includes many important strategies that an effective teacher should be using to maximize learning for a child with ADHD. The items are drawn from scientific research, professional judgment, and consultation with effective teachers. If you set out to improve a marginal teacher overnight with this checklist, your expectations will be unrealistic, but the information can be of help in determining teacher placement for students with ADHD and consulting with teachers who are having difficulties.

1. Does the teacher introduce lessons by setting the stage of learning? Some educators call this "getting ready to learn" or "anticipatory set." The student will be cued that an important lesson is coming and will be more likely to attend.

2. Does the teacher review how he or she expects the student to behave during the lesson?

3. Does the teacher let the student know what he or she should be learning from the lesson?

4. Does the teacher review and recall prior learning from earlier lessons?

5. Does the teacher question the student's understanding of the lesson from time to time?

6. Does the teacher allow "wait time," which gives the student a chance to think about the answer?

7. Does the teacher move about the room during instruction and notice cues that the student is having difficulty, without waiting for the student to initiate a request for assistance?

8. Does the teacher give advance warning that the lesson is about to end and make sure that the student clearly understands the assignment for the following day?

9. Does the teacher instruct the student in how to begin preparing for the next activity and help him or her transition smoothly?

10. Does the teacher supplement classroom instruction with "direct instruction" (structured presentations with much choral repetition of answers with the teacher)?

11. Does the teacher use techniques such as partner reading and peer tutoring to give the student special help?

12. Does the teacher introduce special strategies, such as mnemonic devices, that provide reminders about grammar, punctuation, and pronunciation?

13. Does the teacher teach basic computation with kinesthetic techniques, such as "Touch Math," a special procedure for touching and counting "touchdowns" on the numerals 1 through 9?

14. Does the teacher follow lectures with hands-on activities?

15. Does the teacher use programmed materials that require correction before the student proceeds to the next activity?

16. Does the teacher anticipate problems and plan ahead to avoid them?

17. Does the teacher accept responsibility for ongoing communication with parents?

18. Does the teacher provide ongoing cues to help the student with ADHD return to task and avoid becoming overaroused?

WHAT WORKS IN THE CLASSROOM?

There is no foolproof methodology or strategy that will work with all students with ADHD all of the time. Each student is different depending on the severity of the symptoms, environmental factors, and possible accompanying disabilities (e.g., learning disabilities or emotional difficulties). And what works during the first 3 weeks of the month may have lost its charm by the 4th week. The ADHD Intervention Checklist shown in Form 5.1 includes a variety of strategies and interventions that a teacher might use to help a student with ADHD be more successful academically, socially, and behaviorally. This checklist gives you and your staff a systematic way of determining what adaptations have been tried and with what degree of success. Sometimes, educators approach helping students with ADHD with the same degree of impulsivity and distractibility that their students exhibit. We implement something new for a day or two, keep no records of our progress, and then bemoan our lack of effectiveness. Or we try to implement seven adaptations simultaneously and are doomed to failure before we begin. The most effective teachers have already built many of these strategies into their instructional repertoires and use them with all students. But novice and less effective teachers will need coaching and encouragement to modify their instructional techniques.

WHAT CAN THE PRINCIPAL DO
IF A TEACHER IS UNCOOPERATIVE?

Thankfully, there aren't many Whining Winifreds, Complaining Clydes, or Helpless Hannahs teaching in our schools, but only one can ruin a school year (or even a school career) for a child with ADHD. I'm talking about the "terrible teacher." This pathetic soul is overburdened, overworked, and can reel off more excuses for why he or she can't meet a child's needs than words that the student with ADHD misspelled on his or her last test. Here are just a few of the litany of excuses that will pour forth from the uncooperative teacher's mouth whenever you suggest ways to help a specific student. You'll be able to be more sympathetic to this teacher's negativity and reluctance, however, if you remember the real reason behind this teacher's wall of resistance—fear. He or she is afraid of not being able to teach or manage the student. Students with ADHD threaten an insecure teacher's self-esteem and confidence. With a little coaching and help, however, the reluctant teacher can usually be turned around. Believing that "all teachers can teach," is just as important as believing that "all students can learn." Here are some typical responses you might get.

Blowing Smoke.

This response serves to change the subject from one student's specific needs to the needs of all of the children in the entire world. Well, you don't care about all of the children in the world at that particular moment. You just want one student to learn to read or to stop getting kicked out of class during mathematics or to have an assignment modified to a reasonable level. "I believe in well-behaved students," the teacher will say with a smug smile. Who can argue with that? "I believe that all students should be able to learn in a classroom." The hidden message is, of course, that if you, the principal, would make this student behave and learn, the teacher could do his or her job.

Your reply: "I believe in well-behaved students and learning for all as strongly as you do. That's why I want to support *you* in creating an environment in *your* classroom that will accomplish that for this student. Right now, we have one misbehaving student who isn't learning. What can we do *together* to change that?"

Inadequate Supplies and Materials

This is a favorite excuse of a teacher who doesn't want to meet the needs of a child or more probably is afraid he or she can't. The teacher mistakenly assumes that special materials are needed to teach ADHD students and doesn't realize that "the wizard is really within him or her."

Your reply: "What supplies and materials do you need to do the job? I'll see that you get them." (If this is a genuine need, you can always find money to buy materials. It's usually just an excuse, however, and your response will quickly remove that as an obstacle).

Rigid Standards

More traditional and established teachers frequently have a problem with changing long-standing past practices. They are well-intentioned and often effective teachers but feel that changing their grading method or assignment criteria to meet a single student's needs is somehow "breaking district rules."

Your reply: "I agree with you, Mrs. Smith, that changing your grading system might be perceived as giving Johnny special treatment. Would you agree, however, that our goal is for Johnny to learn? (Hopefully, she'll answer in the affirmative.) If that's the case, Mrs. Smith, then your grading system is standing in the way of Johnny learning. He will never be motivated or encouraged to learn (with his disability) under your present system. Could we just try a brief pilot program or an experiment to see if he might be more motivated and eventually measure up to your standards if you were more lenient for a short time?"

Ignorance

The teacher pleads ignorance and helplessness. "I've never had a student like this before. I haven't had the training yet."

Your reply: "I have some excellent reading material that might give you insight into Johnny and his problems. (At this point, hand her photocopies of the strategies, interventions, and checklists from this book.) I've spoken to the director of pupil personnel services, and she has promised to get you into the first available training spot. I also have some excellent video tapes on ADHD and educational interventions that work. When would you like to borrow them?"

Personality Clash

"I just can't work with this child. He's impossible!"

Your reply: I know how difficult he can be at times. But he really likes you a lot. His mother says he wants to have you over for lunch next week." This might take a miracle to pull off, but you can always try!

Blaming the Child

"Johnny is just going to have to get his act together. He's not going to make it through fifth grade if he doesn't start coming to class on time (or stop talking to his friends, or turn in his assignments)."

Your reply. "I agree that Johnny must be responsible and account-able for his behaviors. But a child with ADHD needs a lot more structure and firmer rules and consequences than the average child in your class. What can we do to tighten the accountability between home and school? Would you be willing to complete a daily assign-ment sheet that he'll bring home every day?" (See Forms 5.2 and 5.3 for examples.)

Passing the Buck

"The school psychologist (or behavior management specialist) is really trained to work with students like this. Maybe Johnny could use some counseling. I just don't have the expertise."

Your reply: "I'm pleased to hear that you feel so positively about the support staff in our building. When could we meet with the psychologist (or counselor) to put together a plan for Johnny?"

Overburdened and Overworked

"There are only so many hours in the day and I've got 35 students. Plus I'm working on my master's degree."

Your reply: "I know how hard teachers work, and I'm really appreciative of all you do. How about a little bargain? If you'd be willing to implement this behavior management plan with Johnny (see Forms 5.4 and 5.5), I'll provide a parent volunteer to duplicate your handouts and tests for the next 2 months."

Blaming the Parent

"I must say, Mrs. Smith, in my 30-some years of teaching, I've never encountered a ruder child than Johnny. His parents could use a class or two on how to discipline their kids."

Your reply: "Parenting a child with ADHD is one of the most challenging assignments a parent will ever have. I don't pretend to know all of the answers, but I do know that poor parenting is not one of the accepted causes of ADHD. His parents have agreed to work on his behaviors at home, and I believe that if Susie knows that you and her parents are working together rather than at odds, it would defi-nitely increase the chances of our success. Would you be willing to try developing a plan together?"

This Is Strictly a Medical Problem

"This kid needs some Ritalin™." The teacher who responds in this way believes that a pill will "cure" ADHD.

Your reply: "Medication is one possible option, but only with appropriate educational interventions can this child achieve to his or her potential. Medication might help, but it has to be administered in conjunction with support from both home and school."

"I Can't Do That. It Wouldn't Be Fair!"

Modifying a grading system, decreasing the workload, or allowing a child with ADHD to take a test orally are practices that seem to strike some teachers as unfair. They are hung up on the concept of fairness being the same thing as equality.

Your reply: "We actually don't do the same thing for every child." Use the analogy that Ross Reed uses:

> These children with ADD have difficulty controlling attentional processes and behavior without help. For them to learn and behave better, they need to experience a high rate of success. They need people to respond favorably to them much more often than unfavorably: perhaps 80% to 90% is an appropriate goal for responding.[5]

UNDER WHAT CONDITIONS SHOULD A CHANGE IN TEACHER PLACEMENT BE CONSIDERED FOR A STUDENT WITH ADHD?

Although it is certainly no secret that inappropriate or mismatched instruction can contribute to and even exacerbate the inattention, impulsivity, and hyperactivity of a child with ADHD, changing an instructional setting (at least from one regular classroom to another) during the course of the school year rarely happens. We administrators are reluctant to admit (except perhaps behind the most tightly closed doors) that we often care more about the feelings of teachers and their unions than we do about students and their learning. Decisions about student placement should ideally be made before the school year begins, but often, new students arrive and are arbitrarily placed in the next available slot, resulting in a poor match of teaching and learning styles, a personality conflict of gigantic proportions, or a "problem teacher" who is ill-suited to dealing with a "problem child." When you have exhausted every approach with an ineffective teacher, don't be hesitant to change a teacher placement, whether within your school setting or by transferring the student to another school in your district. These decisions will, of course, never be made alone. The PPS team or TAT will make the recommendation together. Just be prepared for some raised eyebrows in the faculty lounge. Also, remember whose side you're on.

WHAT DOES EVERY TEACHER NEED?

Teachers are mere mortals, who, when faced with a classroom of 30-plus students, many of whom have special learning needs, often seem short-tempered and frustrated. The child with ADHD is no doubt one of several students who will require curricular modifications and behavioral management plans, so be ready and willing to do some empathizing with the classroom teacher as you make specific requests and recommendations for students with ADHD. If the needs of your classroom teachers are not being met, work with central office administrators and other district personnel to bring about change.

A report of the Michigan Department of Education ADHD Task Force identified 12 specific needs teachers have for support with regard to students with ADHD:[6]

1. The need to be trained in the nature of the handicapping condition, strategies and interventions, medication effects and side-effects, classroom management, and other pertinent information

2. The need to participate in educational planning

3. The need for a speedy and appropriate evaluation on students referred for ADHD evaluations

4. The need to receive assistance and support from school administration

5. The need for support-staff assistance, including at least one individual designated and trained in each building to act as a resource person

6. The need for adequate resources to meet the needs of students with ADHD.

7. The need to have adequate time for planning, coordination, and collaboration

8. The need for a collaborative exchange of information

9. The need for class size reduction considerations when students with severe ADHD are assigned to a class

10. The need for clear, district-level written policy or guidelines

11. The need for a flexible curriculum, which allows for the needs of all students.

12. The need to have adequate parent information available, such as books, videos, handouts, and parent workshops.

WHAT IS THE HIGHEST PRIORITY?

The teacher is the key to school success for the student with ADHD. For 9 months of the calendar year, most students with ADHD will spend their waking hours behind the closed doors of one or more classrooms. The thousands of interactions that take place in those hours will shape the academic self-concept of that student and to a large measure, determine his or her school success or failure. Listen to Jennifer Beacon reflect on her fifth-grade experience:

My fifth-grade teacher called me lazy. I remember not being able to understand a problem right. She wouldn't show me how to do it. I had to figure it out on my own. When I came back lots of times, she got angry and broke her ruler on her desk. She yelled at me and told me I never paid attention and I was lazy and stupid. I never told my mom this because I wanted my mom to think I was smart.

You, as the principal, bear a large measure of responsibility for what happens behind the closed classroom doors. You hire, supervise, mentor, observe, and evaluate each teacher in your building. You encourage, facilitate, suggest, and even cajole. Your mere presence in the classroom is credited with raising achievement test scores.[7] Insist that your faculty meet the needs of students with ADHD, and then, empower them to do the job.

NOTES

1. Adapted from B. G. Burcham and L. B. Carlson. "Attention Deficit Disorder: School-Based Practices." *Executive Summaries of Research Syntheses and Promising Practices on the Education of Children with Attention Deficit Disorder.* Washington, DC: U.S. Department of Education, Office of Special Education and Rehabilitative Services, 1993.

2. Adapted from Maurice McInerney. *Effective Practices for Educating Children with Attention Deficit Disorder,* p. 2. Washington, DC: Chesapeake Institute, 1994.

3. E. K. McEwan. (1997). *Seven Steps to Effective Instructional Leadership.* Thousand Oaks, CA: Corwin Press.

4. John Taylor. *Helping Your Hyperactive/Attention Deficit Child,* p. 157. Rocklin, CA: Prima Publishing and Communications, 1994.

5. Mary Fowler, as quoted in the CH.A.D.D. *Educators Manual: Attention Deficit Disorders,* p. 35. Fairfax, VA: Caset Associates, 1992.

6. Michigan Department of Education. *Attention Deficit Hyperactivity Disorder: ADHD Task Force Report,* p. 62. Lansing, MI: Michigan Department of Education, 1993.

7. Richard Andrews and Roger Soder. "Principal Leadership and Student Achievement." *Educational Leadership, 43,* March 1987, pp. 9-11.

FORM 5.1

ADHD Intervention Checklist

Name_____ School Year _____ Grade _____

| Begin Date | End Date | | Degree of Success |

Environmental Interventions

_____ _____ 1. Assign student to classroom that is structured, consistent, and predictable. _____

_____ _____ 2. Seat student where most visual distractions are behind him or her (e.g., in front row with back to rest of class).[1] _____

_____ _____ 3. Seat student away from potential distractions (e.g., heaters, air conditioners, high traffic areas, pencil sharpeners, windows, water coolers, noisy classmates, etc.). _____

_____ _____ 4. Seat student near teacher as well as appropriate role models. Avoid isolating the student. _____

_____ _____ 5. Post a few simple rules in highly visible places in the classroom. _____

_____ _____ 6. Create a stimuli-reduced area that all students may use (e.g., study carrel in corner of room). Encourage student to self-select this environment when necessary. _____

_____ _____ 7. Permit student to stand, move between two desks, or sit at a round table and move from chair to chair while working. _____

_____ _____ 8. Provide brief breaks (e.g., to run errands, water plants, distribute materials) or exercise breaks to relieve the "wiggles."[2] _____

NOTE: Adapted with permission from Lisa York and West Chicago District #33. Permission has been granted for this publication only and does not extend to reproductions made from this publication. The ADHD Intervention Checklist may be purchased under separate cover for classroom use.

Begin Date	End Date		Degree of Success

_____ _____ 9. Permit student to use earplugs or headphones to block auditory distractions during tests or independent seat work. _____

_____ _____ 10. Allow for a higher level of restlessness and movement on the part of the student during teacher presentation than would normally be acceptable.[3] _____

_____ _____ 11. Other _____ _____

_____ _____ 12. Other _____ _____

_____ _____ 13. Other _____ _____

Academic Interventions

_____ _____ 14. Experiment with a variety of testing formats to find the one best suited to the student's learning style (e.g., true-false, fill-in, multiple choice, or oral). _____

_____ _____ 15. Provide lined answer spaces for responses on short answer or essay tests. _____

_____ _____ 16. Permit student to take tests in less distracting environment (e.g., resource room, study carrel). _____

_____ _____ 17. Permit short breaks during tests. _____

_____ _____ 18. Teach student test-taking strategies (e.g., eliminating all incorrect responses on a multiple-choice test rather than rushing to choose a correct answer).[4] _____

_____ _____ 19. Give student as much time as needed to complete a test. Avoid timed tests whenever possible.

Begin Date	End Date		Degree of Success
_____	_____	20. Provide student with cloze notes to use during lesson presentations. The cloze technique provides student with an outline or set of notes with key words missing. The student is expected to fill in missing key words during direct instruction.	_____
_____	_____	21. Provide photocopied text or an outline on which student can underline or highlight key concepts during direct instruction.	_____
_____	_____	22. Provide ample "wait time" (i.e., the amount of time you wait for an answer during classroom discussions). Allow at least 5 seconds. Return to student if he or she needs more time to organize a verbal response.	_____
_____	_____	23. Show student examples of completed assignments that demonstrate the teacher's expectations (e.g., research projects, book reports, essays, dioramas, or stories).	_____
_____	_____	24. Provide student with audiotape of important text material.	_____
_____	_____	25. Permit student to highlight main ideas in textbooks and jot notes in margins.	_____
_____	_____	26. Encourage the use of a word processor for preparation of assignments.	_____
_____	_____	27. Permit alternate methods for note taking (e.g., photocopy the notes of a more organized student, permit the student to compare his or her notes with those of another student, or allow student to copy the notes of the teacher).	_____

Begin Date	End Date		Degree of Success
_____	_____	28. Schedule more demanding classes or subjects when student is at peak performance.	_____
_____	_____	29. Emphasize quality of assignment rather than quantity (e.g., three well-constructed sentences are preferable to not handing in the assignment at all).	_____
_____	_____	30. Make eye contact with student before giving instructions. Ask student to restate instructions before beginning independent practice.	_____
_____	_____	31. Teach, model, and frequently reinforce one specific previewing or comprehension strategy and encourage the student to practice and use it consistently (e.g., SQ3R).[5]	_____
_____	_____	32. Give a concrete reinforcement, such as a star or token, for the completion of each in-class assignment.	_____
_____	_____	33. Enlist the help of an aide or volunteer to read important material aloud to the student.	_____
_____	_____	34. Allow the student to dictate thoughts and ideas to someone else before copying his or her dictated information.	_____
_____	_____	35. Give student several options for both obtaining and reporting information (e.g., audio- or videotapes, interviews, reading, experiences, projects, displays, oral presentations, photographic essays, conference with teacher, field trips, etc.).	_____

Begin Date	End Date		Degree of Success

_____ _____ 36. Permit the use of a calculator to check accuracy of math computation. _____

_____ _____ 37. Other _____ _____
_____

_____ _____ 38. Other _____ _____
_____

_____ _____ 39. Other _____ _____
_____

Instructional Interventions

_____ _____ 40. Vary lesson presentations between those requiring student to sit still and listen with those that are more visual or participatory. _____

_____ _____ 41. Modify curriculum (e.g., choose an easier reading level or require fewer or easier spelling words). _____

_____ _____ 42. Use an interactive teaching approach that introduces the same information to the student through each of the senses. _____

_____ _____ 43. Use strategies that cue student as to the expected learning outcomes (e.g., maps, charts, outlines, preview questions, study guides, or vocabulary lists to focus student's attention on key information). _____

_____ _____ 44. Devote some instructional time each day to the teaching or reviewing (or both) of memory, reading, organizational, or behavioral strategies. _____

_____ _____ 45. Structure lessons in a logical and sequential fashion. Minimize instructional "bird walks," which lose or confuse the student. _____

Begin Date	End Date		Degree of Success
_____	_____	46. Keep directions brief, logical, and sequential.	_____
_____	_____	47. Summarize key information more frequently and check for understanding by asking student(s) to respond physically (e.g., thumbs up, thumbs down).	_____
_____	_____	48. Provide periodic breaks in longer lesson presentations.	_____
_____	_____	49. Use the overhead projector to focus student's attention (e.g., frame important information, reveal a step-by-step process, use different colors and shapes, or involve the student in writing on the transparency).	_____
_____	_____	50. Give student verbal and visual clues in anticipation of introducing important information or key concepts.	_____
_____	_____	51. Use computer-based drills and instruction to provide practice and to reinforce basic skills.	_____
_____	_____	52. Use proximity to the student during a lesson presentation to increase interaction and to hold his or her attention.[6]	_____
_____	_____	53. Develop private signals with student to focus his or her attention (e.g., wink, point to ears or eyes, touch top of head).	_____
_____	_____	54. Use the unison response method for increased student attention and participation (e.g., individual chalkboards or magic slates, or yes-no class responses, such as thumbs up or down or open hand, closed hand).	_____

Begin Date	End Date		Degree of Success
_____	_____	55. Make frequent direct eye contact to gain and hold student's attention during lesson presentation.	_____
_____	_____	56. Present more difficult subjects or tasks to the student when performance is at peak (e.g., first thing in the morning, 2 hours after medication has been given).	_____
_____	_____	57. Teach memory strategies, such as mnemonics, frequent written or spoken repetitions, visualization, or oral rehearsal.	_____
_____	_____	58. Use the "turn to your partner" technique during the lesson presentation to help the student summarize what he or she has learned or to refocus attention.	_____
_____	_____	59. Teach student specific information-locating strategies (e.g., how to use textbooks, reference books, skimming and scanning, and card catalog).	_____
_____	_____	60. Develop a classroom or subject matter reference book that contains frequently used vocabulary or spelling words, rules, procedures, checklists, and mathematical formulas.	_____
_____	_____	61. Keep a folder containing the student's best work as a comparative standard against which to evaluate future performance.	_____
_____	_____	62. Evaluate all instructional handouts to make sure they are well-designed and clearly written. Avoid any material that is poorly photocopied, handwritten, or in tiny type.	_____

Begin Date	End Date		Degree of Success
_____	_____	63. Develop specific and consistent classroom routines to facilitate learning and organization (e.g., how to get help when student has questions, where to turn in completed assignments, what to do when free time is available, etc.).	_____
_____	_____	64. Make sure student comprehends task before permitting him or her to begin independent work (e.g., repeat the directions to the teacher or another student, write down the steps, or highlight the directions on a handout as they are read aloud).	_____
_____	_____	65. Teach mathematical processes using manipulatives and real-world examples.	_____
_____	_____	66. Visually display commonly used mathematical formulas. Show examples in a step-by-step format or develop a checklist.	_____
_____	_____	67. Use daily oral activities (e.g., one math problem-solving activity; one language activity, one memory technique per day) to reinforce skills.	_____
_____	_____	68. Visually display the most commonly used problem-solving strategies in mathematics.[7]	_____
_____	_____	69. Use graph paper for math computation to keep numbers in columns.	_____
_____	_____	70. When working story problems, have the student underline key words and phrases.	_____

Begin Date	End Date		Degree of Success

_____ _____ 71. Other _____ _____
                           _____
                           _____

_____ _____ 72. Other _____ _____
                           _____
                           _____

_____ _____ 73. Other _____ _____
                           _____
                           _____

Organizational Interventions

_____ _____ 74. List all special classroom events for the week or month on a large calendar and periodically refer to them to assist student with long-term planning. _____

_____ _____ 75. Give student a few minutes at the end of each subject or class to organize books, papers, and so on, before beginning next instructional sequence. _____

_____ _____ 76. Give student extra set of books to increase the likelihood that texts will always be available when needed. Keep one at school and one at home. _____

_____ _____ 77. Use color-coded materials to help student keep organized (e.g., folders, sticky notes, xeroxing on different colors of paper). _____

_____ _____ 78. Require that the student have individual notebook or folders for each subject. Help the student index them. _____

_____ _____ 79. Notify parent(s) immediately of missing or incomplete assignments. _____

Begin Date	End Date		Degree of Success
_____	_____	80. Develop a reward-and-consequence system for both in-school work and homework completion.	_____
_____	_____	81. Assist student to develop a system to keep track of completed, partially completed, and corrected work (e.g., folders, notebook, baskets, etc.).	_____
_____	_____	82. Provide frequent reminders (both written and verbal) of due dates for assignments.	_____
_____	_____	83. Divide lengthy, long-range assignments into steps, and provide intermediate deadlines for the completion of each step.	_____
_____	_____	84. Develop checklists for common classroom assignments (e.g., writing a book report, composing an essay, doing a long-division problem). Tape these lists to the desk or keep them in a notebook where they are easily accessible.	_____
_____	_____	85. Develop checklists for common classroom procedures (e.g., arriving at school, getting ready to go home).	_____
_____	_____	86. Establish, display, and maintain a daily classroom routine and schedule. Explain changes to the schedule well in advance.	_____
_____	_____	87. Monitor clutter on the student's desk. Make sure the desktop is free from all material except that on which he or she is working.	_____

Begin Date	End Date		Degree of Success
_____	_____	88. Have the student clean out and reorganize his or her desk or locker at regular intervals. Ask the student to purchase a desk or locker organizer to assist.	_____
_____	_____	89. Check notebooks and folders weekly to make sure completed work has been turned in and graded assignments have been taken home.	_____
_____	_____	90. Write all assignments for the day on a chalkboard or flip chart. Use color, graphics, and humor to keep this area interesting.	_____
_____	_____	91. Provide a time at the end of each day for the student to reorganize his or her desk and homework materials. Designate a "coach" or "buddy" to help with this organizational checkpoint.	_____
_____	_____	92. Have student cross items off a list when completed to promote a sense of accomplishment.	_____
_____	_____	93. Systematically teach organizational skills to student, focusing on the skills before the subject matter.[8]	_____
_____	_____	94. Teach student to monitor and record his or her own work productivity and behavior.	_____
_____	_____	95. Other _____ _____ _____	_____
_____	_____	96. Other _____ _____ _____	_____

Begin Date	*End Date*		*Degree of Success*
_____	_____	97. Other _____ _____ _____	_____

Homework Interventions

_____	_____	98. Go over assignments that will be going home using both auditory and visual presentations whenever possible (e.g., chalkboard, overhead, or handouts).	_____
_____	_____	99. Ask student to restate homework expectations or read them aloud from his or her assignment notebook before leaving classroom.	_____
_____	_____	100. Allow extra time for student to copy assignments.	_____
_____	_____	101. Develop a homework buddy system in which the buddies monitor each other to make sure the assignments are understood and all necessary materials are taken home. Encourage buddies to exchange telephone numbers.	_____
_____	_____	102. Require the regular use of an assignment notebook. Include columns for assignment, date due, and date handed in. Inspect and initial each day. As student learns routine and becomes more consistent, sign once per week.	_____
_____	_____	103. Require periodic status reports on long-term assignments.	_____
_____	_____	104. Provide a step-by-step sequence of intermediate steps when giving the student a complex assignment.	_____
_____	_____	105. Frequently review and reinforce successful homework strategies in cooperative groups.[9]	_____

Begin Date	End Date		Degree of Success
_____	_____	106. Monitor the writing down of homework assignments.	_____
_____	_____	107. Send daily or weekly progress reports home.	_____
_____	_____	108. Eliminate all "busywork" homework assignments; include only material that is absolutely necessary to practice or learn.	_____
_____	_____	109. Use highlighter markers or "neon" sticky tabs to indicate to the student where to start or stop an assignment or where important information can be found.	_____
_____	_____	110. Reduce the amount of homework initially to achieve small increments of success, and then gradually increase expectations as confidence increases.	_____
_____	_____	111. Permit the student to submit work as soon as it is completed.	_____
_____	_____	112. Give feedback on all completed homework assignments.	_____
_____	_____	113. Have frequent, even if short, one-to-one homework conferences with student to assess completion rate, quality of work, and problems he or she may be having.	_____
_____	_____	114. Assign a peer to help the student with homework.	_____
_____	_____	115. Allow the student additional time to turn in homework assignments.	_____
_____	_____	116. Send homework assignments and materials home with someone other than the student (e.g., sibling or neighbor).	_____

Begin Date	End Date		Degree of Success

_____ _____ 117. Provide ample guided practice for the student prior to giving home-work assignment(s).   _____

_____ _____ 118. Other _____   _____
                        _____
                        _____

_____ _____ 119. Other _____   _____
                        _____
                        _____

_____ _____ 120. Other _____   _____
                        _____
                        _____

Behavioral Interventions

_____ _____ 121. Design an individual behavior management plan suited to the student's unique needs.[10]   _____

_____ _____ 122. Use a timer to help student stay on task. He or she can be rewarded when he or she beats the timer.   _____

_____ _____ 123. Structure positive ways student can receive attention from teacher (e.g., classroom or leadership responsibilities).   _____

_____ _____ 124. Establish a secret signal to remind the student to return to task. Praise the student when he or she is on task.   _____

_____ _____ 125. Implement a cognitive behav-ioral modification or therapy program to encourage a self-monitoring approach on the part of the student.[11]   _____

Begin Date	End Date		Degree of Success
_____	_____	126. Have student chart his or her own instances of appropriate or inappropriate target behavior (e.g., hand raising, on-target conversation or interruptions, swearing).[12]	_____
_____	_____	127. Give the student choices when possible (e.g., to decide whether to work on math or reading assignment).	_____
_____	_____	128. Give specific praise for desired behavior, taking care to give more praise than reprimands.	_____
_____	_____	129. Keep reprimands brief and directed at unwanted behavior rather than at the student.	_____
_____	_____	130. Develop classroom rules with student discussion and input.	_____
_____	_____	131. Teach classroom rules as if they were subject matter. Role-play examples of excellent behavior. Give student(s) opportunities for practice. Test knowledge of rules. Review rules regularly.	_____
_____	_____	132. Set hourly, daily, weekly, or monthly goals with the student, and provide frequent feedback on the student's progress.	_____
_____	_____	133. Develop a hierarchy of consequences.[13]	_____
_____	_____	134. Teach "stop, listen, think, say, do" strategy to reduce impulsivity.	_____

Social Skills Interventions

Begin Date	End Date		Degree of Success
_____	_____	135. Use positive practice to reinforce desired skills.	_____

Begin Date	End Date		Degree of Success
_____	_____	136. Praise appropriate social behavior more frequently than reprimanding inappropriate behavior. Tally the incidence of each.	_____
_____	_____	137. Set up social behavior goals with student, and implement a reward program.	_____
_____	_____	138. Prompt appropriate social behavior either verbally or with a private signal.	_____
_____	_____	139. Teach prerequisite skills for cooperative learning (listening, accepting feedback, praising, giving feedback), and use this technique in classroom when appropriate.[14]	_____
_____	_____	140. Implement a social skills program either with the individual student or with the entire class.[15]	_____
_____	_____	141. Reinforce social skills training in natural settings (e.g., playground, lunchroom).	_____
_____	_____	142. Assign special responsibilities to student in presence of peer group so others observe the student in a positive light.	_____
_____	_____	143. Use group rewards as an incentive (e.g., use "hero" technique in which one student earns a reward for the entire class).	_____
_____	_____	144. Change reinforcers frequently to maintain interest and motivation. Consult with student regarding choice of reinforcers.	_____

Begin Date	End Date			Degree of Success
_____	_____	145. Other	_____ _____ _____	_____
_____	_____	146. Other	_____ _____ _____	_____
_____	_____	147. Other	_____ _____ _____	_____

Notes and Resources For Table 5.1

1. Intervention #2: This seating arrangement could have its disadvantages because the student will lose the opportunity to pick up visual cues from classmates regarding appropriate attending behaviors and what textbooks and materials are being used. Consider a seat near the front rather than in the front row as another option.

2 Intervention #8: Encourage student to use seat isometrics, such as pushing feet down on floor or pulling up on the bottom of the chair.

3. Intervention #10: If the classroom teacher is personally sensitive to distractions and movements, associates stillness with attentiveness, or believes that the student is purposely annoying the teacher, educate the teacher regarding the needs of the student with ADHD for movement to aid in concentration.

4. Intervention #18: *Parents' Guide to Solving School Problems: Kindergarten Through Middle School* (Harold Shaw, 1995) and *"The Dog Ate It": Conquering Homework Hassles* (Harold Shaw, 1997) by Elaine K. McEwan contain a variety of test-taking strategies that can be taught to students.

5. Intervention #31: *Solving School Problems: Kindergarten Through Middle School* (Harold Shaw, 1995) by Elaine K. McEwan contains a variety of comprehension strategies that can be taught to students.

6. Intervention #52: Long and Newman's "Managing Surface Behavior of Children in School, " in N.J. Long, W. C. Morse, and R.G. Newman (Eds.), *Conflict in the Classroom: The Education of Children With Problems,* Fourth edition, pp. 233-241 (Wadsworth, 1980) describes five different levels of proximity control: (a) orienting one's body toward a student, (b) walking toward a student, (c) putting one's hand on the student's desk, (d) touching or removing the object used by a student to create distraction, or (e) putting one's hand gently on a student's shoulder or arm. Note that care must be taken when personally touching a student, however, because some students react negatively to touch.

7. Intervention #68: *Parents' Guide to Solving School Problems: Kindergarten Through Middle School* (Harold Shaw, 1995) by Elaine K. McEwan contains a variety of mathematical problem-solving strategies that can be taught to students.

8. Intervention #93: Sandra Rief, in *How to Reach and Teach ADD/ADHD Children: Practical Techniques, Strategies, and Interventions for Helping Children with Attention Problems and Hyperactivity* (The Center for Applied Research in Education, 1993, p. 45) suggests that students should be taught how to organize their material, organize their work place, record their assignments, make lists, prioritize activities, plan for short-term assignments, break down long-term assignments, know the standards of acceptable work, read and use a calendar, read a clock and follow a schedule, know what to take home and leave home, know what to take home and return, know when and where to turn in assignments, know what to do specifically during seat

work time, know what to do when seat work is completed, and know what materials are needed and expected.

9. Intervention #105: A variety of excellent materials to teach cooperative learning techniques to both teachers and students can be obtained from Interaction Book Company, 7208 Cornelia Drive, Edina, MN 55435 (612-831-9500).

10. Intervention #121: See Ginger Rhode's, *The Tough Kid Book: Practical Classroom Management Strategies* (Sopris West, Inc., 1992) for hundreds of ideas on structuring classroom management for challenging children. (1-800-547-6747.) Possible programs include behavior contracts, cost-reward systems (student earns points, tokens, chips, etc., for desired behavior as well as losing tokens, etc. for undesirable behavior), and cost-response systems (student starts day with all the points, tokens, etc., and has to work to keep them).

11. Intervention #125: See Lauren Braswell and Michael Bloomquist's, *Cognitive Behavioral Therapy With ADHD Children: Child, Family, and School Interventions* (The Guilford Press, 1991).

12. Intervention #123: *Making It Work on Monday* by Susan L. Fister and Karen A. Kemp (Sopris West, 1995) contains "countoons, " ready-made charts with cartoon characters on which students can count their appropriate and inappropriate behaviors. (1-800-547-6747.)

13. Intervention #134: Mary M. Kerr and C. Michael Nelson (*Strategies for Managing Behavior Problems in the Classroom.* New York: Macmillan, 1989) have suggested a range of negative consequences that have been found to be effective: (a) use of soft reprimands, (b) in-class time-outs (e.g., sending to corner of room or outside door of room), (c) changing a preferred seat location, (d) taking away privileges (e.g., free time, class helper status), (e) taking away points or tokens that may have been earned, (f) during-school detention (e.g., during activity or elective periods), (g) before-school or after-school detentions, (h) restitution activities (e.g., repaint the room, repair a chair, replace a pen), (i) parent telephone calls or conferences, (j) time-outs or conferences with principal, (k) recording a poor score on behavior for grading class participation or work habits or both. Other possible negative consequences that might be included in the hierarchy include (a) head down on desk, (b) time in school office, (c) in-school suspension, and (d) out-of-school suspension.

14. Intervention #139: See note 9 for Intervention #105.

15. Intervention #140: Possible choices include Dowd and Tierney's *Teaching Social Skills to Youth: A Curriculum for Childcare Providers* (Boystown Press, 1992) and their companion book for students, *Basic Social Skills for Youth: A Handbook From Boystown*, Camp and Bash's *Think Aloud: Increasing Social and Cognitive Skills: A Problem-Solving Program for Children* (Research Press, 1981), and Ginger Rhode's *The Tough Kid Social Skills Book* (Sopris West, Inc., 1995).

FORM 5.2

Weekly Assignments Form

Daily assignments for week beginning (date)_____

Name Teacher/Homeroom _____

	Monday	*Tuesday*	*Wednesday*	*Thursday*	*Friday*
Reading					
Math					
Spelling					
English					
Social Studies					
Science					

Teacher Comments: _____

_____

_____

Parent Comments: _____

_____

_____

FORM 5.3

Daily Progress Report

Name _____ Date _____

How was I in class today?

0 = Terrible, 1 = Fair, 2 = Good, 3 = Excellent

Behavior	Class Periods						
	1	2	3	4	5	6	7
Prepared for class (book, pencil, paper)							
Followed directions							
Completed in-class work							
Handed in homework							
Cooperative with teacher							
Worked without disturbing others							
Paid attention							

Teacher comments (e.g., explain what the student did well; reasons for an extremely negative rating; what assignments need to be completed)

Parent comments (e.g., identify consequences given for this report, i.e., TV, phone friends, treats, Nintendo, points in behavior program, or loss of privileges)

Parent Signature _____

Return to teacher, with parent signature, to receive a new progress report.

<u>**FORM 5.4**</u>

Behavior Evaluation Form,
Sample #1

Name: _____

Date now: _____

Time now: _____

Date when behavior occurred: _____

Time when behavior occurred: _____

Location where behavior occurred: _____

Adults present when behavior occurred: _____

What were the *expectations?*

1.

2.

3.

4.

5.

What was *your behavior?*

Was your behavior *appropriate or inappropriate?*

Why did you do what you did?

What was your goal?

How did you feel while it was happening?

How will you handle the situation next time?

How do you feel now?

Are you ready to be appropriate with the class?

FORM 5.5

Behavior Evaluation Form,
Sample #2

Name: _____

Date: _____

Time: _____

What was expected of you?

Use positive words

Use positive body language

Follow directions

Raise my hand before speaking

Stay in my seat

Hand in my homework

Keep objects out of my hands

Do not throw things

Did you understand what you were supposed to do?   Yes   No

What did you do?

Talked

Whispered

Teased

Complained

Laughed

Threw something

Rolled my eyes

Giggled

Got out of my seat

Did not turn in my homework

Tattled

Disrupted a lesson

Played

Made a noise

Did you do the right things?   Yes   No

NOTE: Reprinted by permission of the author, Jane Skaggs. Readers may reproduce this document for their professional use.

Why did you do it?
Bored
Angry
Afraid
Forgot
Lonely
Confused
Mad
Sad
Excited
Copied others
Wanted to be noticed
Wanted it my way
Feeling tired
Feeling sick
Being silly
Wanted to leave
Trying to get even

Do you feel this way often?   Yes   No

What do you plan to do next time?
Sit quietly
Raise my hand
Ignore others
Tell the teacher
Ask for help
Ask for time out
Count to 10
Tell an adviser
Talk with a friend
Move my seat
Move away
Think of my choices
Think of the consequences
Do my work
Follow directions
Mind my own business

Do you think this plan will work?   Yes   No

Are you going to follow the plan?   Yes   No

6

HELPING PARENTS COPE

Words of Wisdom for Frustrated Families

When one family member struggles with ADD, every other family member is also a victim of its influence. We all "suffer" from ADD in the Beacon household.

—Karen Beacon

Not one of my three sons would ever be considered "easy" by anyone's standards. Needless to say, the boys [two of them with ADHD] take everything out of me by the end of each day. They require that I be healthy and energized at all times, full of patience, tolerance, and a tremendous sense of humor. The parenting job is monumental. ADHD has taken over our lives—if not consciously, then certainly subconsciously. There is just no ignoring the situation for one second of the day.

—Vivian Martinelli

I know that as a building principal, you probably don't have a diploma in marriage and family therapy, but that doesn't stop parents from cornering you in the hallway when they're looking for someone who will listen to their problems. Although poor parenting and shaky marriages don't cause ADHD, they can certainly exacerbate these common characteristics of family life. And the very presence of a child with ADHD can make even the most idyllic home seem a little crazy at times. To further confound family life, 25% of the fathers and

19% of the mothers of children with ADHD have ADHD themselves as adults. You don't have to wonder why 16% of the mothers of children with ADHD suffer from depression and dysthymia (despondency and chronic melancholy) in addition to their decreased sense of competence. Families that live with ADHD on a daily basis need a lot of encouragement, and as a building principal, you are in a position to offer it. They also need large doses of communication, coordination, and consistency between home and school. The suggestions that follow are ones that I have shared with hundreds of parents in my roles as teacher, principal, author, and radio and television show guest on the topic of parenting. Feel free to adapt them and make them your own as you counsel and encourage the families in your school.

WHAT'S THE BEST ADVICE A PRINCIPAL CAN GIVE PARENTS?

Perhaps the parents with whom you counsel will listen in disbelief if you share too much of your "proverbial wisdom," so sometimes what I call "wordless advice" works best. Wordless advice means you simply listen as a parent shares with you what is happening at home. As you nod, ask some of the questions I've posed in the sections ahead. Perhaps by the end of your session, the parent may have gained a better understanding of the issues and may even be ready to listen to some of the advice that follows. Or better yet, just photocopy the pages and share them.

Is the pace of your home so hectic and out of control that there is little time for reflection and communication? A busy book editor periodically takes stock of her frenetic two-career household when things seem to be spinning out of control. She can usually pinpoint that she hasn't been spending time with her daughter who has ADHD and that the hugs and positive strokes have been few and far between. "I often find that simply slowing down long enough to give my children some extra feedback goes a long way towards helping them want to cooperate with me."

Another parent echoes this theme: "An atmosphere of peace and stability is important. Routine and regularity of schedules are also. We are constantly reevaluating our priorities."

Streamline and organize your home. Try to keep mealtimes, bedtimes, and other schedules as predictable as possible. Learn to say "no" to those who call with requests for your time. If you have any leftover time, use it for yourself.

Are you modeling the behaviors that you desire to see in your children? Although your child may be inattentive, he or she has an uncanny ability to discover the inconsistencies between what you say and what you do. Remember to "walk your talk" as consistently as possible. If you become angry, critical, frustrated, and manipulative in dealing with your child, count on getting the same behaviors back in kind. Children do, indeed, "learn what they live" as that well-known poem so eloquently describes.

Are you forgetting to "accentuate the positive" while trying to "eliminate the negative"? Encouragement and incentive are the most powerful tools for change. Reward your child externally with attention and concrete external motivators. Don't fall into the trap of thinking your child "should" behave because it's the right thing to do or because behaving will make him or her feel good. Forget that line of reasoning altogether. Children, especially those with ADHD, don't think like that. When you fall into the trap of thinking they do, you'll spend a lot of time being angry at your child for his or her irresponsibility and lack of self-discipline. Responsibility and self-discipline will take years and years of hundreds of positive and successful experiences rewarded by your affirmation and recognition. Charlene Bryne suggests that you spend some time with parents of "normal" children as well. "It helps to realize that all kids are weird! Not everything is ADHD."

Are you trying to fit your "round child into a square hole"? Rather than accepting your child's limitations, are you trying to turn him or her into a quiet and model child? Relax. Provide lots of outlets for excess energy. Avoid gatherings where your child is bound to get into trouble. Don't let your child get a bad reputation in the family or neighborhood. Protect him or her from sharp-tongued aunts and nosy neighbors. Recognize that your child has a genuine disability and cannot always help his or her behavior without strong support and intervention from all of the significant adults in his or her life. Support your child. Listen to him or her. Love and accept your child.

Do you have a clear understanding of the basic principles of human behavior? The first and most important principle of human behavior is simply this: Children behave the way they do to get our attention. And they will try to get what they want regardless of the consequences.

The best and most effective classroom teachers use this principle well and wisely. They don't wait for students to misbehave to give them attention; they meet them at the door with a smile, a word of greeting, and a pat on the back. Find ways to give your child positive attention before he or she does something negative and you find it almost impossible to be positive. Your child wants to be loved, accepted, and noticed by you more than anything in the whole world. Even your negative attention is better than nothing. Be certain you are noticing and affirming the right things.

Are you inconsistent and wishy-washy in following through? This single mom speaks for many parents of ADHD children when she bemoans her lack of consistency in discipline: "Sometimes I feel so exhausted, it's easier to let my son do what he wants. Reality discipline and time-outs work well—*when* I follow through." Have a few, clear, consistent rules. Don't waste your breath on negative comments, such as "Don't do that," or "Stop that." Enforce the rules with time out, loss of privileges, or other consequences that your management plan sets forth. Get all the help you need on child management. Parents who go through child management courses and use the skills they learn have children who are better adjusted than parents who do not attend or who do attend and don't use the skills.

I've developed the following 10 commandments for behavior management of children with ADHD (they also work well with other kids) and I "preach" them wherever I go. The wording is my own. The concepts and principles have been adapted from Whitman and Smith[1] and John F. Taylor.[2]

First Commandment:
Thou Shalt Have Clearly Defined Lines of Authority.

Your child needs to know who's in charge, what the rules are, and what happens when the rules are broken. These guidelines will make life safe, predictable, and stable for your child who inwardly is experiencing chaos on a daily basis. Get your collective acts together (as husband and wife) and always present a united front to your child.

Second Commandment:
Thou Shalt Not "Go With the Flow."

Children with ADHD need predictability and routine constantly. The more consistent you can be regarding bedtimes, mealtimes, procedures for getting dressed, leaving for school, and doing homework and chores, the easier your life will be. Spend time getting yourself, your household, and your child organized. Spend time teaching organizational strategies to your child. Then, don't deviate from them. Children with ADHD have a difficult time dealing with any kind of change. If they are expending their energies coping with a fluid lifestyle at home, they will have a very difficult, if not impossible, time accomplishing any of their own tasks at school.

Third Commandment:
Thou Shalt Always Think and Plan Ahead.

As annoying as it is to constantly be thinking ahead, it is an essential skill for managing life with ADHD. Overplan and you can't go wrong. Think about how your child responds in supermarkets, restaurants, and church. Then decide what props (snacks, coloring books, quiet toys) will be needed to manage. Warn your child of upcoming changes in the schedule or situations that will be different than anything he or she has encountered before. Rehearse and role play behavior if necessary.

Fourth Commandment:
Thou Shalt Communicate.

To be effective, communication must be assertive. Clearly expressing your ideas and requests to your child in a direct and reasonable way sets the stage for a long-term relationship based on trust. Some parents feel guilty at being so direct and assertive with their children. It's easy for this kind of parent to be manipulated by an argumentative or uncooperative child. The permissive parent frequently asks the child whether he or she would like to do something rather than giving a direct command. Just as debilitating to the management system, however, is a punitive, threatening, and harsh approach to communication. Either extreme on the continuum will result in an unfortunate backlash of behavior. Assertive communication exhibits patience, self-control, firmness, and clarity.

Fifth Commandment:
Thou Shalt Not Obfuscate.

You may not be familiar with this rather obscure verb, but it's perfect for this context. *Obfuscating* means obscuring, confusing, or muddling. And that's precisely what many parents do when giving directions to their children or setting forth behavioral expectations.

Make sure that whenever you communicate with your child, whether it be regarding cleaning his room or apologizing to her brother, that you give explicit and specific directions. Children with ADHD cannot "fill in the blanks" or "read between the lines." They need to have it spelled out exactly. Put it in writing, make a list, explain it verbally, draw some simple pictures, or make a chart. Don't leave it to chance.

Sixth Commandment:
Thy Consequences Shall Be Constructive and Logical.

Consequences are what happens to your child after he behaves or misbehaves. Consequences that require restitution or contribution always work best. When I was an elementary school principal, I specialized in these kinds of consequences. Always with parental permission, I would frequently assign physical work tasks, such as cleaning washroom walls or picking up trash on the playground. Sitting in detention hall or writing sentences (typical elementary school consequences) frequently only resulted in further punishments being heaped on the student. They couldn't sit still or stay on task at 3:30 after a long day at school, and repeated writing was doubly painful. Work (although it required a different kind of supervision) kept them active, moving, and productively engaged. I often worked alongside to provide a role model. One parent I know discovered that work can be a very effective consequence:

> Grounding doesn't work on ADD kids. I'll go to the mat on that one. All you do is ground yourself, and it doesn't produce any better grades or behavior. It only torments everyone involved. It only further isolates the child from normal family life when what he needs is a tremendous amount of acceptance. Giving a child an extra chore not only is a disciplinary step, but gives him something to do to burn off some energy.

Seventh Commandment:
Thou Shalt Be Consistent.

Consistency means always doing the same thing in the same situation. Children with ADHD will constantly test the limits. They will test them far more persistently than other children. The more often the child is unsure of what the parental response will be or if there will be any response at all, the more frequently he or she will test the limits. Only by exhibiting consistency can you help your child begin to develop internal controls on his or her impulsivity. He or she will eventually decide that misbehaving is not worth what will happen to him or her when he or she does "that."

Eighth Commandment:
Thou Shalt Continually Provide Supervision.

Children with ADHD cannot be left unsupervised, even when they reach ages where common sense would tell you they could function on their own. It just doesn't work that way, and you'll regret it if you don't follow this commandment. You might find your child swinging from the chandelier or destroying your prize collection of Faberge eggs if you become complacent. Consider the example of this parent:

Dustin (almost 12) is not the kind of child I can leave alone for an afternoon while I run errands or take a nap. Dustin is a real "Ferris Bueller" who never ceases to come up with unusual new schemes. In the same way that I monitor Dustin's free time, I also monitor his homework time. I help him to divide and conquer his work and to pace himself for the evening as he accomplishes harder tasks. For Dustin, idle time means boredom and boredom means trouble.

Ninth Commandment:
Thou Shalt Not Become Angry, Vindictive,
Hostile, Argumentative, or Physically Abusive.

Although we've all done it—lost our temper, spanked our child, shouted out in frustration and anger—we know it doesn't work. Once we've lost control of ourselves, we've most definitely lost control of our child. If this happens, pick up the pieces, apologize, and regroup. Using physical punishment, such as spanking, is much less effective than any of the other techniques we have mentioned. Physical punishment rarely has the desired long-term effect and often causes emotional difficulties, such as fear, worry, deep sadness, or even increased disobedience in children. Modeling physical aggression when that is often the behavior we are trying to extinguish just doesn't make sense.

Tenth Commandment:
Thou Shalt Affirm, Support, Redirect, and Educate.

Never lose an opportunity to give your child some positive strokes. The more positive input your child can receive, the more positive output he will be able to produce. Learn to empathize verbally with your child by making statements such as, "I understand how you feel," "How can I help you so you'll feel better?" or "Tell me more about how you feel." Always be ready to step in and redirect your child to another activity if boredom, fatigue, loneliness, or irritability are boiling over. Vivian Martinelli believes it is important for her to "deactivate" her son Dustin intellectually, physically, and creatively each day:

> My son's psyche is on constant overdrive and must be "drained" daily or he can't sleep at night. I complement his school curriculum with books, rental movies, trips to museums and exhibitions, theater, and even travel. I try to keep up with and saturate his ever-racing mind with new information and problems to consider. I send him on fact-finding missions to the CNN news, newspapers, encyclopedias, and the library.

Are you trying to do it all on your own? Seek out assistance from support groups, school and community agencies, religious organizations, friends, and family. You cannot parent a child with ADHD alone.

Are you neglecting your spouse and marital relationship? Get help for marital problems ASAP.

WHAT ARE THE BENEFITS OF FAMILY COUNSELING?

In addition to the possibility of medical therapy as described in Chapter Four and the educational interventions detailed in Chapter Five, a child's treatment plan might also include family education and counseling. Education for the family is important for two reasons: Total involvement of the family serves to take the spotlight off a misbehaving child and shifts it to a child who has a medical problem that needs to be managed. Second, it sets the stage for altered expectations and treatment for the child. Understanding all aspects of ADHD will help the family deal more productively with the problems they encounter. Denial, relief, anger, and grief are all natural stages that families may pass through on their way to a healthy acceptance and proactive stance regarding the diagnosis of ADHD.

Joan Griswold has gone through several stages, not all of them expected:

My first response to the diagnosis was relief to know that there was an explanation for what was happening to my daughter at school and for her behaviors at home (e.g., low tolerance for frustration, emotional lability, and extreme messiness). But now I have begun to deal with the grief, realizing that our daughter is going to struggle with this for a long time and that her options in life may be more limited because of it. The grief took me somewhat by surprise, I must admit.

HOW CAN FAMILY TRAINING HELP?

Training in behavior management and modification is another important component of any treatment program. Without this training, many parents will have a difficult time structuring the home environment, something that is essential for every family member's physical and mental health. Russell Barkley and his staff at the University of Massachusetts have identified eight general principles in the daily behavior management of ADHD children.[3]

1. ADHD children require more immediate feedback or consequences for their behavior and activities than do normal children.

2. ADHD children require these types of behavioral consequences more frequently than do normal children.

3. ADHD children require more salient or substantial consequences than do normal children to motivate them to do work.

4. In modifying the behavior of an ADHD child, it is critical that parents avoid the all-too-common tactic of trying punishment first to suppress unwanted behavior. Put positives before negatives.

5. Consistency is of critical importance to the management of ADHD children. Consistency over time and in different places and settings is crucial.

6. Parents of children with ADHD must try to anticipate problem situations.

7. Keep the right perspective on the behavior problems that may arise.

8. Practice forgiveness.

These principles are not part of the average parent's repertoire of parenting behaviors; training can help.

IS COUNSELING FOR THE CHILD ESSENTIAL?

Many children and young people with ADHD can benefit greatly from individual coaching and counseling. Jennifer Beacon, 14 years old, describes her learning specialist:

> I have a friend named Ruth. She's more than a friend. She is a blessing. Ruth isn't like anybody else I know. She is in her early forties and she is beautiful and strong. Ruth changed me. She helped me become myself and strive to be the best I can. Freshman year, my grades were at a record low along with my self-esteem. My mom heard about her from a friend. Ruthie is a learning specialist, and she is kind of like a tutor. We decided to give it a try. At first, I was upset. An hour and a half a week? Yuck! But then I met Ruth. I never trust adults, never fully at least, but I trusted Ruth, first thing. Throughout that year, Ruth became more than my learning specialist. She became my friend. She taught me how to be organized and how to study for tests and do my homework. She also taught me that I was beautiful inside even though I was different. I soon learned that I was smart and I wasn't dumb. Slowly, my grades came up, along with my self-esteem.

WHAT ARE THE COMPONENTS OF A HOME MANAGEMENT PLAN?

I believe that every family needs a home management plan, but for families living with ADHD, the need is especially critical. A home management plan has the following components: (a) a behavior management plan, (b) a problem-solving model, (c) instruction for the child in self-management and self-talk skills, and (d) a family communication model. Here's how each component works.

Part One: The Behavior Management Plan

The behavior management plan is comprised of a set of rules and expectations for your child and guidelines for what you will do and what will happen to him or her when the rules are not kept. The plan will govern how you discipline your child and how you respond to misbehavior.

Part Two: The Problem-Solving Model

The problem-solving model consists of a several-step process that parents can use with each other and their children to identify and solve common problems. The model should be "practiced" and perfected using neutral dilemmas so that when genuine family problems arise, the skills are in place. A model that I have found helpful in my family and professional life is the following:[4]

Step One: Begin to define the problem. Talk it over and write it down.

Step Two: Gather information. Get input from all of the people involved in the problem.

Step Three: Redefine the problem. The problem may be worse than you thought and have several aspects, or you may discover you really don't have a problem at all.

Step Four: Establish an acceptable outcome. Decide what you want to have happen as a result of solving the problem, and if at all possible, make the outcome measurable.

Step Five: Generate alternative means. Don't just settle for one solution to the problem; your first solution may not work.

Step Six: Establish the plan. Make sure you detail why the plan is being prepared, who is going to participate, what specific actions each individual will take, when these activities will be performed, and where they will occur.

Step Seven: Evaluate the effectiveness of your plan after you have implemented it. If it didn't work, select another alternative.

Many families post these steps on the refrigerator and refer to them during particularly tense situations, either for the child or the family. When Mary Ellen Corcoran occasionally "blows it" due to sheer weariness or a particularly incomprehensible action on Kevin's part, she tries to model problem-solving behavior, thinking out loud about the choice she made, how it worked out, and what other choices she could have made. She is never reluctant to apologize to her children when it's needed.

Part Three: Skill Instruction

Some families find that instruction for their child in self-management and self-instruction helps them develop an internal language of positive self-statements. This type of training is usually offered in clinic settings where professionals focus on a comprehensive treatment plan for children with ADHD and their families. "Talking to oneself" is something that adults do quite automatically. Children are not usually capable of self-instruction until the age of 6 or 7. Examples of positive self-statements that children might learn are "I think I can do it," "If I try, I can be successful," "If I keep working, I'll improve." See Appendix I for home interventions that emphasize cognitive behavioral management. These techniques try to change problem behavior by putting the child in control of the behavior-change plan.

Part Four: The Family Communication Model

The fourth aspect to the home management plan is the development of a family communication model that includes holding periodic family meetings to discuss problems and learn how to resolve conflicts positively.[5] Communication problems that might be addressed include how to handle vague and ambiguous statements, blaming, getting off-topic, dominating conversation, put-downs and destructive verbalizations, interrupting, poor listening and poor eye contact, and incongruent verbal and nonverbal messages. This type of training is most useful when families have older school-aged children or adolescents.

Here is an example of how the Martinellis handle their son with ADHD, age 7, who has been classified as a behavior disordered student at school. His plan has been multifaceted, including lots of parent training courses, counseling, an IEP (individualized education plan) at school, daily visits from the Behavior Disordered Itinerant teacher, a daily progress chart from school, and a reward system for good behavior in school, church, and at sport events. Special play times and poker chip redemption systems have worked well.

His mother doesn't just "hope for the best." She has carefully structured her home and her son's schedule around his needs.

> I run a very carefully supervised household. I try as much as possible to take proactive measures with Cameron so that I can avoid disciplinary problems. I make sure he gets his medicine (Ritalin™) exactly on time, that he doesn't get overtired, and that he gets adequate nourishment (protein, complex carbohydrates, and very little sugar). I supervise his homework closely. I also direct Cameron into safe, constructive activities and choose just the right friends to invite over. I encourage friend-

ships with active children who usually have big brothers also. In other words, I encourage friends who "speak the same language" as Cameron, literally and metaphorically. Sometimes, I need to send Cameron to his room to "chill out" when things get out of hand. This happens less and less now as he grows older. I reward Cameron's good behaviors at school (as identified on a daily progress chart that the teacher sends home) with tokens. He can then redeem his tokens for movie or Sega rentals or trips to a favorite restaurant. I change the rewards regularly to keep them novel and interesting. Cameron has trouble playing with a few of the kids on our street. To avoid any more neighborhood problems, I don't allow him to roam freely around the street. I accomplish this by playing with him myself outdoors (a.k.a. our special play time) or by having his own carefully selected friend over. By doing fun and interesting things on our property, Cameron doesn't get into any problems with the neighbors. I'm ready to do whatever it may take to keep Cameron's life running smoothly. It is almost a 24-hour job, but it's worth it. I never leave things open to chance or leave Cameron to his own desires. His natural instincts are to be extremely reckless, aggressive, rambunctious, and impulsive if he gets overstimulated. To balance these characteristics at home, I hold to very clear limits and low-key activities to keep things in control.

WHAT ELSE CAN YOU DO TO SUPPORT PARENTS?

Here are just a few ways you and your faculty can support parents of students with ADHD:

- Offer training in child management.
- Offer training in the use of cognitive behavior modification (see Appendix I).
- Organize a parent support group, and offer the school building as a meeting place.
- Set up a resource library, and make books and tapes on ADHD available for borrowing (The Council for Exceptional Children offers an excellent starting kit with videos and resource materials for only $50.00 plus $5.00 for shipping and handling).[6]

- Invite parents of successful, older ADHD students to share their experiences.
- Use parents as volunteers and tutors in the classroom.
- Invite a local physician or psychologist to present a program on ADHD.
- Invite the behavior management specialist to share the "tricks of his or her trade" with parents of ADHD students.
- Invite a marriage and family therapist to present a program.
- Subscribe to ADHD newsletters and make them available to parents.
- Organize parent-child communication workshops.
- Purchase or borrow Thomas Phelan's book and video on the 1-2-3 Magic method of child management (see Bibliography) and invite a group of parents to view and discuss them.
- Purchase or borrow Thomas Phelan's book and video on ADHD (see Bibliography) and invite a group of parents to view and discuss them.
- Put together a parent-teacher roundtable to share information about effective behavior management and attention-getting strategies.
- Organize a Megaskills workshop.[7]
- Purchase or borrow Russell Barkley's video series (see Bibliography) and invite a group of parents to view and discuss them.

WHAT'S THE NEXT STEP?

Before you put this book back on your office shelf, don't forget to check out the Resources section. Read the family stories in Resource A. They include more information about the parents and students with ADHD who were quoted throughout the book. Their stories are thought provoking and inspiring. Check out the many organizations and resources in Resource B. Their help is available to those wishing more information about ADHD. Browse through the remaining resources and mark those to which you will return for help in the weeks ahead. And last, make a note in your daily planner to determine where your school and district stand with regard to putting policies and procedures in place that will best serve the needs of students with ADHD. Rather than thinking of this task as just one more thing to do in an already burgeoning "to do" list, consider this task as one that is critical to improving the quality of your entire school and its achievement. "Notching up" instruction for students with ADHD will benefit every student, including those with other disabilities or behavioral difficulties. Slow learners will blossom under many of the interventions and strategies suggested for students with ADHD, and even gifted students will benefit from being taught organizational skills and cooperative learning techniques. You can't go wrong. Begin today.

NOTES

1. Barbara Y. Whitman and Carla Smith. "Living with a Hyperactive Child: Principles of Families, Family Therapy, and Behavior Management." In *Attention Deficit Disorders and Hyperactivity in Children* by P. J. Accardo, T. A. Blondis, and B. Y. Whitman, pp. 187-211. New York: Marcel Dekker, Inc., 1991.

2. John F. Taylor. *Helping Your Hyperactive/Attention Deficit Child*, pp. 324-352. Rocklin, CA: Prima Publishing and Communications, 1994.

3. Russell A. Barkley. *ADHD: What Can We Do?* Program Manual to accompany video, pp. 11-17. New York: Guilford Publications, 1992.

4. Elaine K. McEwan. *Parent's Guide to Solving School Problems: Kindergarten through Middle School*, p. 13. Wheaton, IL: Harold Shaw Publishers, 1992.

5. Rudolf Dreikurs, Shirley Gould, and Raymond J. Corsini. *Family Council: The Dreikurs' Technique for Putting an End to War Between Parents and Children (and Between Children and Children.)* Chicago: Henry Regnery Company, 1974.

6. Council for Exceptional Children, 1920 Association Drive, Reston, VA 20191. 1-800-232-7323 or Fax: 703-264-1637.

7. Contact Dorothy Rich at the Home and School Institute in Washington, DC (202-466-3633) for information on becoming a Megaskills Trainer or holding a Megaskills training for parents in your school.

RESOURCE A:
FAMILY BIOGRAPHIES

Pseudonyms have been used for the families described here. Each family participated in a combination of interviews and the completion of an extensive questionnaire regarding their experiences with ADHD. The family histories are arranged in alphabetical order by last name.

THE ADAMS FAMILY

Brett Adams is the 10-year-old son of Laura and Lyle Adams. He was diagnosed with ADHD (combined) at the age of 7. Brett has two siblings, a 14-year-old brother and an 8-year-old sister. Neither of Brett's parents nor siblings have ADHD, but his maternal grandfather and uncle both have ADHD symptoms that were undiagnosed. Brett takes Imipramine (100 mg) and Ritalin™ (10 mg). He is enrolled in a private school where his teachers are responsive to his needs and modify the curriculum as needed. His parents struggle with discipline at home because Brett is very oppositional, and he also suffers with social problems at school. Brett's ADHD has definitely affected the family's life; they don't get out much because of problems finding baby sitters who are willing to meet Brett's needs for discipline and structure.

154

THE BEACON FAMILY

Jennifer Beacon is the 14-year-old daughter of Karen and Sonny. She has one younger sister, 12. Jennifer was diagnosed with ADHD (with attention deficit) at the age of 10. Although neither of her parents have ADHD, Jennifer's maternal grandfather and his sisters have very severe cases. Karen reports that the outcome was a tragic, loveless home filled with anger, abuse, and great sadness. Jennifer takes Ritalin™ and Tegretol™ (prescribed to treat a general seizure disorder). Until this year, the Beacons have found "stubborn ignorance and unprofessional attitudes" among the educators in their suburban school system. Now, in the high school, they have found knowledgeable administrators and creative and energetic teachers who have put Jennifer's best interests first. Jennifer's grades are marginal, but her interactions with teachers and school experiences are definitely more positive. Jennifer is receiving counseling from a successful professional who also has ADHD, and this experience is proving very beneficial for her self-esteem.

THE BROWN FAMILY

Perry Brown is the 18-year-old son of Helen and Shelby Brown. He is the only male with five sisters, two older and three younger. Perry was diagnosed with ADHD at the age of 12. Although his parents do not have ADHD, Helen reports that her 49-year-old brother shows many symptoms of ADHD. Ritalin™ was recommended for Perry, and although his parents supported this recommendation, he hated it, saying it made him feel weird. After 1 month, he stopped taking the drug. Perry graduated from high school and completed two college courses, but lied about attending a third. Perry is rebellious, oppositional, and irresponsible. His parents found it necessary to ask him to leave their home because of his problems with the law. They took away his car, and he is presently living with an uncle and working a part-time job. He refuses to follow rules and spends most of his time hanging out with friends.

THE BURNS FAMILY

Daniel Burns is the 6-year-old son of Shelley and Bob. He was diagnosed with ADHD (combined) at the age of 4 and has one sibling, a 3-year-old sister. After reading about ADHD and talking with the psychologist who diagnosed Daniel, his father believes he may have ADHD as well. He struggled through school, "feeling out of step with what was going on." Bob's father and maternal grandmother have symptoms similar to both Bob and Daniel. Daniel's parents have decided not to use medication and are trying diet and vitamins. These treatments are difficult to monitor, but his parents believe they could be helping. Daniel has severe problems with insomnia, often waking up for 2 to 3 hours in the middle of the night. Daniel's behavior is a challenge to manage; Shelley and Bob carefully plan where they go to avoid embarrassment at Daniel's behavior. Daniel's current school placement is a frustration for his parents. The teacher believes that "if he just learned to mind," he would be fine. She has felt free to criticize Shelley's parenting skills—"she's too laid back"—and believes that parents use ADHD as an excuse not to discipline their children.

THE BYRNE FAMILY

Brett Byrne is the 29-year-old son of Charlene. Charlene and her second husband have a second child, 23. Brett was diagnosed as hyperactive (the only diagnosis used at the time) at the age of 7. He took Ritalin™ until puberty and then stopped taking the drug because of the doctor's recommendation. His grades fell dramatically at that point, and his mother believes it would have been beneficial to keep him on the drug longer. Charlene worked hard at catching Brett doing things right even though he was a disruptive child. Today Brett is the co-owner of a business, a homeowner, and a responsible and happy adult. His mother reports that he skate boards, snow boards, rides motorcycles, and still needs to go fast. He is a sensitive and loving person and has learned to concentrate when he needs to.

THE CORCORAN FAMILY

Kevin Corcoran is the 9-year-old son of Mary Ellen and Kevin Corcoran. He is the oldest of three boys. Kevin was diagnosed with ADHD at the age of 7 but was treated for anxiety beginning at age 5. Kevin takes both Ritalin™ and imipramine. No other family members have ADHD. Until this year, Kevin's school setting was not ideal; gang shootings were commonplace, and a sexual assault occurred inside the school. School personnel did not cooperate in the administration of medication, and Kevin was once thrown out of school for his lunchroom behavior. Since moving to a new neighborhood, he is in a structured classroom in a well-run school where everyone works together to meet his needs. His parents are thoughtful and energetic individuals who are constantly working on new interventions and run a "tight ship."

THE DIXON FAMILY

Jacob Dixon is the 10-year-old son of Janet and Joe Dixon. He is the middle child between two other boys. He was diagnosed at the age of 7 and takes Ritalin™. His mother has experimented with eliminating sugar and preservatives in Jacob's diet but has seen no changes in his behavior at all. No other family members have ADHD. Jacob's schooling experiences have been mixed. He also has a learning disability, and his mother reports that the Learning Disabilities teacher is condescending and demeaning to both her and Jacob. She is grateful to many other school personnel for making her aware of her child's problems and for the work they have done to help Jacob. She believes that Jacob's successes are "due to the 'real teachers' and that the others should find a new line of work."

THE GRISWOLD FAMILY

Joanna Griswold is the 10-year-old daughter of Joan and Robert Griswold. She was diagnosed with ADHD without hyperactivity when she was 9 years old. Joanna's father has ADHD symptoms. She is one of two daughters, and there is a great deal of sibling rivalry and fighting between the girls. Joanna takes Ritalin™, and her mother credits the drug with Joanna's improved ability to follow through and complete projects for school without constant monitoring. Joanna is most fortunate to have a wonderful teacher; she receives A's and B's and loves school. The teacher works with Joanna each term to set new goals. They have worked on doing assignments more thoroughly and neatly, and now they are working on speaking up in class. The teacher goes way beyond the call of duty, according to Joan, who credits her for the success her daughter is having. Joanna's ability to concentrate, get along with family members, and deal with frustration is nearly gone by the afternoon hours, so evenings are a challenge in the Griswold household.

THE HARRIS FAMILY

Matt Harris is the 19-year-old son of Lori and Tom Harris. He is the youngest of three children, and his siblings have graduated from college and married. Matt was diagnosed with ADHD (without hyperactivity) at the age of 15. Tom believes he, himself, was borderline ADHD but was able to compensate for the symptoms because of his high level of interest and aptitude in both math and science. Matt's older brother was very impulsive but extremely gifted. His teachers seemed to accept his behavior as part of his giftedness. After his ADHD diagnosis and Ritalin™ treatment, Matt had a successful 2 years in high school. His parents believed that perhaps he had been "cured." Matt tried a year away at a college of his own choosing, but the unsupervised and unstructured experience was not successful. He then returned home and attended a community college. With this successful experience behind him, he will now attend a college that offers special programs for students with ADHD and learning disabilities. His parents are confident that in this atmosphere, he will be successful.

THE KINGMAN FAMILY

Brent Kingman is the 6-year-old son of Sue and Charles Kingman. He has recently been diagnosed with ADHD and has just begun taking Ritalin™. He is the youngest of three children. Brent is in kindergarten and is learning his academics, but he is a discipline problem and has a short attention span. The teacher says she is "on him all the time." Brent creates problems for his family with his demanding and intolerant ways. He constantly talks, makes noises, and finds ways of getting attention. His parents are working to develop a more consistent approach to discipline and family structure.

THE KINGSTON FAMILY

Danny Kingston is the 11-year-old son of Monica and Greg Kingston. He was diagnosed with ADHD (without hyperactivity) at the age of 10. Danny has responded extremely well to Ritalin™ during the day, but by the time he comes home from school, the "wailing and gnashing of teeth" begins. Danny's 14-year-old brother has a "rare love" for him and seldom lacks patience with Danny's antics. Greg Kingston definitely feels that he personally suffers from ADHD. He expresses empathy toward Danny, reliving the pain he often felt in childhood. He continues to have many frustrations today. Monica believes that she may also have a tendency toward ADHD. Her early report cards indicate distractibility and fidgeting. Danny's teachers seem overworked and burdened by several children with ADHD and whine about the difficulty of taking time for the needs of each child. Monica feels that she is "just another mom with a problem child" and has requested a reassignment for Danny to a school where children like Danny are accommodated. But she feels fortunate to have an educator-husband who has experience with children like Danny and knows how to interpret district policies, procedures, and "lingo."

THE KIRKPATRICK FAMILY

Jameson Kirkpatrick is the 6-year-old son of Linda and James Kirkpatrick. He has just been diagnosed with ADHD. Ritalin™ has been recommended. Jameson is one of five children, a sister, 25, and three brothers, 19, 14, and 2. Linda believes that she may have ADHD. She had a hard time staying on task and finishing things in school. Because she was an adopted child, she has no knowledge of her relatives. She is currently in counseling to help her with the general organization and discipline of her home. Linda has found school personnel to be extremely helpful in developing an individualized education plan for Jameson and providing materials and suggestions for a home discipline program. Linda's biggest challenge with Jameson is that he thinks the living room is an outdoor soccer field and gymnasium. He is always running, jumping, skipping, hopping, and rolling.

THE MARSHALL FAMILY

Donna and Ryan Marshall have three children, Matthew, 11, Rachel, 9, and Sandra, 7. They all were diagnosed with ADHD in the past year. Both Donna and her husband have all the symptoms of ADHD, although they have never been formally diagnosed. There are indications, however, on both sides of the family. Donna's brother and father have symptoms. Ryan's brother and cousins also have symptoms. All three children are on Ritalin™ with great success. Donna reports that mornings are the most challenging for the Marshall family.

Imagine five ADHD people with poor memories. No one can remember what they were doing or where they put their shoes. We daydream far too long without getting dressed and hair combed. Rachel can forget she is taking her medicine with it right in front of her. Mornings are a battlefield.

But ADHD has strengthened the Marshall family, and their wonderful sense of humor keeps them going. Donna looks for teachers who love children, but school can be a nightmare, she reports. She fights for her kids but does become exhausted and gives up for moments here and there.

THE MARTINELLI FAMILY

Dustin and Cameron Martinelli are the 11-year-old and 7-year-old sons of Vivian and Bob Martinelli. Dustin was diagnosed with ADHD at the age of 8 and Cameron at the age of 4. Vivian's response when Cameron was diagnosed was "Not again! Why me?" Both boys take Ritalin™, but Vivian believes that a multifaceted program is very important—parent training courses, counseling, daily progress charts at school, and a reward system for good behavior in school, church, and at sporting events. Dustin's intelligence has given him an edge at school, and Vivian volunteers regularly. She credits her heavy involvement with the smooth road that Dustin has experienced in school. Cameron has more severe behavior problems in school and needs the "ideal" teacher. The principal has been difficult to work with in this regard. But this year, Cameron is finally experiencing success in the classroom. The Martinellis have been in counseling but have experienced frustration in finding just the right person. Vivian reports that the therapist must be one who specializes in ADHD, and the search for a good counselor can be costly and emotionally draining.

THE MONTGOMERY-CASTRO FAMILY

Israel Castro is the 10-year-old son of Miriam Montgomery, a single parent. He was diagnosed with ADHD at the age of 8, much to his mother's relief. The blame for his behavior had been laid heavily on the shoulders of Miriam by family members and school officials. Miriam believes her ex-husband has ADHD, and her older son who lives with his father exhibits many of the same characteristics. Since taking Ritalin™, Israel's behavior has changed drastically. He is more calm. Miriam experienced a great deal of frustration with school personnel until Israel's diagnosis. They sent Israel home from school 2 days a week or sent him to another classroom. As a result, he was held back a grade. Since the diagnosis, she has been able to insist on more specific instruction for him, and teachers seem more patient now.

THE O'BRIEN FAMILY

John is the 14-year-old son of Patricia and Robert O'Brien. He was diagnosed with ADHD at the age of 10. Patricia can trace several ADHD indicators in her family tree. She reports that on her mother's side, "all the men were a little crazy but nothing more specific was ever said." Robert feels that he has ADHD symptoms that were never diagnosed. Although his parents resisted medication at first, life at home became a nightmare, and in desperation, Patricia called the pediatrician. She reports that the first week John was on the medicine, he was able to attend church and not come home upset. John was able to sit for the entire hour without excessive talking, noises, drumming on the pews, and tapping his feet. She got no stares and looks from the people sitting around her. She believes God was letting her know that giving her son the medicine was the right thing. She still believes this today. Up to this year, he had been doing very well in school—A's and B's. But high school has been a different story. Placed in the highest level academic classes in his freshman year, he has encountered teachers who refuse to accept his diagnosis and one who accused his parents of "drugging him into a zombie." Patricia advises not to let the school pass the ball back to parents but to force them, with repeated contact, to deal with the issue.

THE REASOR FAMILY

Jeff Reasor is the 9-year-old son of Bruce and Marilyn Reasor. He was diagnosed with ADHD at the age of 6. Bruce believes that he may have ADHD, but no other family members exhibit symptoms. Jeff has been taking Ritalin™ since his diagnosis with outstanding success. His parents have structured their home, eliminated as many distractions as possible, and use time out very effectively. One of three children, Jeff is experiencing a high level of success in school. He is part of the Gifted and Talented Program, and his parents find school personnel very willing to listen and work with them. Teachers are knowledgeable about ADHD and are eager to learn and share information. Bruce and Marilyn agree that a "triple dose of patience" is needed when raising a child with ADHD.

THE ROLLINS FAMILY

Christopher and Cindy Rollins are 9 and 6. Their mother, Kandi, is divorced and lives with her parents. Christopher was diagnosed with ADHD at the age of 6 and his sister at the age of 5. Christopher has been taking Ritalin™ since kindergarten, and doctors are still experimenting to find the right dosage and combination for Cindy. There are many family members on both the maternal and paternal sides who have ADHD symptoms. Both children attend a private Christian school. Christopher is a straight-A student, but Cindy is suspected of having minor learning disabilities in reading and spelling. The familylike atmosphere at the school and the care of the teachers have contributed to a wonderful school experience for the Rollinses.

THE SCOTT FAMILY

Billy and Phillip Scott are the 12-year-old and 10-year-old sons of Jane and Richard Scott. Billy was diagnosed with ADHD at the age of 7.

His original diagnosis was for an anxiety disorder, and when treatment for 8 months with therapy was not entirely successful, he was diagnosed with ADHD and began a treatment of Ritalin™. This drug caused some side effects, and so Billy began taking Cylert™, which did not prove effective either. Now, he is taking Adderol™ (a Dexedrine™ derivative that is currently in short supply) and his mother reports, "it is working great." Phillip is more compliant and easygoing than Billy, and this causes charges of favoritism from Billy. Both parents have multiple ADHD symptoms. Jane has been officially diagnosed and is taking slow-release Ritalin™ with great success. Although Richard has never been officially diagnosed, Jane reports that he is impulsive, easily distracted, and hyperactive. Denial of his symptoms causes severe marital stress. He is easily frustrated, fails to understand why the children behave as they do, and has on occasion reacted physically toward the children. Jane has stated that if this occurs again, she will seek a separation from him. Billy receives support services in school, and although he is in accelerated math class, he has been close to failing two other subjects. Jane is in constant contact with the school and has encountered her greatest frustration in understanding the assignments given to the boys at school. The support services teacher has been the greatest help, with keeping assignments updated, working with the regular teachers to complete a daily reporting sheet, and allowing previous missed assignments to be turned in.

THE SULLIVAN FAMILY

Raymond is the 8-year-old son of Maxine and Raymond Sullivan. He was diagnosed at 1 year, which is an unusually early diagnosis. No other family members have ADHD symptoms, but Raymond was decidedly different from his two older siblings in sleep patterns, eating habits, activity level, and concentration level. He began taking Ritalin™ in first grade, and this was successful for about a year until he suddenly developed tics. Now, the doctor is trying Wellbutrin™. Raymond is an uncooperative child who is very moody, and his behavior has affected the Sullivan's marriage adversely. Although he has been identified as a special education student, Raymond is "included" in the regular education classroom with extra help. Maxine works closely with school personnel and finds them supportive. She just feels a little guilty that they have to deal with Raymond's problems all day every day.

THE TYRONE FAMILY

Jeffrey Tyrone is the 14-year-old son of Rosemary and Walter Tyrone. Jeffrey was diagnosed with ADHD at the age of 13. He has one older sister, 18, who is "average." Although he had always had trouble in school with behavior and his mother suspected there might be something wrong, the combination of an interested teacher and a radio program on ADHD motivated Rosemary to seek professional attention. Before he began to take Ritalin™, Rosemary reports that Jeffrey told her that life wasn't worth living. "He seemed to change right before my eyes." Rosemary believes that she has ADHD. She has the same feelings her child has but thinks that because she is a female, she has had an easier time compensating for her disability. She still looks for shortcuts for everything and hated school, except for the social part. Jeffrey seems to handle only one challenge well at a time. If he's managing school, he's a grouch at home and vice versa. His mother fights to keep him from being "pushed through the cracks" at school. Although he has a special education label, he is mainstreamed (in regular classes), except for math. Rosemary keeps the lines of communication open with the school and goes to them, not as an irate parent but as a concerned parent interested in her child's welfare. Jeffrey's behavior is a constant strain on the Tyrone's marriage. Before Jeffrey was diagnosed, Rosemary believes she almost lost her family and marriage. Jeffrey seems to be the ground for "fighting" between husband and wife. Walter is starting to understand ADHD and Rosemary understands all too well, having been there.

THE WALKER-HUNT FAMILY

Josh Hunt is the 14-year-old son of Bonnie and Laird Walker. He was diagnosed with ADHD at the age of 10. Josh has two older brothers, and although they do not have ADHD, Bonnie reports they are both strong willed. The oldest has been hard on Josh and very unaccepting of his behavior. Although he takes Ritalin™, Josh doesn't like it, and his parents aren't totally sold on it either. It does seem to help though. They tried beginning two school years without the medication and then had to start using it. Josh is a challenging child in the area of discipline, and his mother's passive personality and stressors at home combine to create a less than favorable situation. Laird would like Bonnie to be firmer and exact more follow-through on consequences. Josh recently transferred from a large public junior high school to a small (100 student), very structured Christian school. He was doing very poorly in the public school. Bonnie believes that many teachers pay lip service to understanding ADHD but are either unwilling or unable to adapt their teaching strategies to meet the child's needs.

THE WOODS FAMILY

Darrell Woods is the 7-year-old grandson of Brian and Kristen Woods. He was diagnosed with ADHD at the age of 6. The Woods have legally adopted Darrell because his mother (the Woods's daughter) has severe mental problems. The Woodses have other children, including a son with spina bifida. Darrell takes Ritalin™, which has been effective in helping him attend to tasks. Darrell will start school in the fall, and his grandparents are in a quandary about where to send him. They don't see public education in their area as a positive choice, but private school is prohibitive financially. Although the Woodses have sought counseling, insurance only pays for "desperation times." Their budget does not permit additional visits.

RESOURCE B:
ORGANIZATIONS
AND RESOURCES

ORGANIZATIONS FOR INFORMATION, SUPPORT, AND ADVOCACY

Attention Deficit Disorder Association (ADDA)
P.O. Box 972
Mentor, OH 44061
1-800-487-2282

Attention Deficit Information Network (AD-IN)
475 Hillside Avenue
Needham, MA 02194
617-455-9895

CH.A.D.D. (Children and Adults With Attention Deficit Disorders)
National Headquarters
499 NW 70th Avenue
Suite 308
Plantation, FL 33317
305-587-3700
(CH.A.D.D. has local chapters throughout the United States. Locations, contact names, and phone numbers are available through National Headquarters).

Council for Exceptional Children
1920 Association Drive
Reston, VA 22091-1589
703-264-9474
1-800-328-0272
FAX 703-264-9494

Health Resource Center (National Clearinghouse for
    Postsecondary Education for People With Disabilities)
1 DuPont Circle N.W.
Washington, DC 20036

Learning Disabilities Association
4156 Library Road
Pittsburgh, PA 15234
412-341-1515

National Center for Learning Disabilities
99 Park Avenue
New York, NY 10016
212-687-7211

NICHCY (National Information Center for Children and Youth
    With Disabilities
P.O. Box 1492
Washington, DC 20013
1-800-695-0285

DISABILITY RIGHTS
ADVOCACY ORGANIZATIONS

Bazelon Center for Mental Health Law
1101 15th Street N.W.
Suite 1212
Washington, DC 20005-5002
202-467-5730
202-467-4232 TDD

Center for Law and Education, Inc.
955 Massachusetts Avenue
Cambridge, MA 02139

DREDF (Disabilities Rights Education and Defense Fund, Inc.)
1616 P Street N.W.
Suite 100
Washington, DC 20036

National Council on Disability
800 Independence Avenue S.W.
Suite 814
Washington, DC 20591
202-267-3846
202-267-3232 TDD

NPND (National Parent Network on Disability)
1600 Prince Street
Suite 115
Alexandria, VA 22314
703-684-6763
(NPND has a listing of parent networks throughout the United
States. They will mail or fax it to you upon request.)

UNITED STATES GOVERNMENT

For questions about IDEA
and PL 94-142, call or write to

U.S. Department of Education
Office of Special Education Programs
400 Maryland Avenue S.W.
Washington, DC 20202
202-205-5507

For questions about Section 504,
call or write to

U.S. Department of Education
Office for Civil Rights
400 Maryland Avenue S.W.
Washington, DC 20202
202-732-1635

For questions about Americans
with Disabilities Act (ADA),
call or write regarding discrimination to

> EEOC (Equal Employment Opportunity Commission)
> 1801 L Street N.W.
> Washington, DC 20507
> 1-800-669-4000

Regarding accommodations, call or write to

> United States Department of Justice
> Civil Rights Division
> P.O. Box 66118
> Washington, DC 20035-6118
> 1-800-669-3362

DEPARTMENT OF EDUCATION OFFICE FOR CIVIL RIGHTS REGIONAL CIVIL RIGHTS OFFICES

Region I: Connecticut, Maine, Massachusetts,
New Hampshire, Rhode Island, Vermont

> Regional Civil Rights Director
> Office for Civil Rights, Region I
> U.S. Department of Education
> John W. McCormack Post Office and Court House-Room 222
> Post Office Square
> Boston, Massachusetts 02109
> 617-223-1154
> TTY 617-223-1111

Region II: New Jersey New York,
Puerto Rico, Virgin Islands

> Regional Civil Rights Director
> Office for Civil Rights, Region II
> U.S. Department of Education
> 26 Federal Plaza, R33-130
> New York, NY 10278
> 212-264-5180
> TTY 212-264-9464

Region III: Delaware, District of Columbia,
Maryland, Pennsylvania, Virginia, West Virginia

    Regional Civil Rights Director
    Office for Civil Rights, Region III
    U.S. Department of Education
    Gateway Building, 3535 Market Street
    Post Office Box 13716
    Philadelphia, Pennsylvania 19101
    215-596-6772
    TTY 215-596-6794

Region IV: Alabama, Florida, Georgia, Kentucky,
Mississippi, North Carolina, South Carolina, Tennessee

    Regional Civil Rights Director
    Office for Civil Rights, Region IV
    U.S. Department of Education
    101 Marietta Tower, Room 2702
    Atlanta, Georgia 30323
    404-221-2954
    TTY 404-221-2010

Region V: Illinois, Indiana, Minnesota,
Michigan, Ohio, Wisconsin

    Regional Civil Rights Director
    Office for Civil Rights, Region V
    U.S. Department of Education
    300 South Wacker Drive, 8th Floor
    Chicago, Illinois 60606
    312-353-2520
    TTY 312-353-2520

Region VI: Arkansas, Louisiana,
New Mexico, Oklahoma, Texas

    Regional Civil Rights Director
    Office for Civil Rights, Region VI
    U.S. Department of Education
    1200 Main Tower Building, Room 1935
    Dallas, Texas 75202
    214-676-3951
    TTY 214-767-6599

Region VII: Iowa, Kansas, Missouri, Nebraska

Regional Civil Rights Director
Office for Civil Rights, Region VII
U.S. Department of Education
324 E. 11th Street, 24th Floor
Kansas City, Missouri 64106
816-374-2223
TTY 816-374-7264

Region VIII: Colorado, Montana, North Dakota,
South Dakota, Utah, Wyoming

Regional Civil Rights Director
Office for Civil Rights, Region VIII
U.S. Department of Education
Federal Office Building
1961 Stout Street, Room 1185
Denver, Colorado 80294
303-884-5695
TTY 303-844-3417

Region IX: Arizona, California, Hawaii, Nevada,
Guam, Trust Territory of the Pacific Islands, American Samoa

Regional Civil Rights Director
Office for Civil Rights, Region IX
U.S. Department of Education
1275 Market Street, 14th Floor
San Francisco, CA 94103
415-556-9894
TTY 415-556-1933

Region X: Alaska, Idaho, Oregon, Washington

Regional Civil Rights Director
Office for Civil Rights, Region X
U.S. Department of Education
2901 3rd Avenue, Mail Stop 106
Seattle, Washington 98121
206-442-1636
TTY 206-442-4542

RESOURCE C:
U.S. DEPARTMENT OF
EDUCATION POLICY STATEMENT

UNITED STATES DEPARTMENT OF EDUCATION
OFFICE OF SPECIAL EDUCATION AND
REHABILITATIVE SERVICES

MEMORANDUM   THE ASSISTANT SECRETARY

DATE: September 16, 1991

TO: Chief State School Officers

FROM: Robert R. Davila
               Assistant Secretary
               Office of Special Education
                  and Rehabilitative Services

               Michael L. Williams
               Assistant Secretary
               Office for Civil Rights

               John T. MacDonald
               Assistant Secretary
               Office of Elementary and Secondary Education

SUBJECT: Clarification of Policy to Address the Needs of Children with
Attention Deficit Disorders Within General and/or Special Education

I. INTRODUCTION

There is a growing awareness in the education community that attention deficit disorder (ADD) and attention deficit hyperactive disorder (ADHD) can result in significant learning problems for children with these conditions.[1] While estimates of the prevalence of ADD vary widely, we believe that three to five percent of school-aged children may have significant educational problems related to this disorder. Because ADD has broad implications for education as a whole, the Department believes it should clarify State and local responsibility under Federal law for addressing the needs of children with ADD in the schools. Ensuring that these students are able to reach their fullest potential is an inherent part of the National education goals and AMERICA 2000. The National goals, and the strategy for achieving them, are based on the assumptions that: (1) all children can learn and benefit from their education; and (2) the educational community must work to improve the learning opportunities for all children.

This memorandum clarifies the circumstances under which children with ADD are eligible for special education services under Part B of the Individuals with Disabilities Act (Part B), as well as the Part B requirements for evaluation of such children's unique educational needs. This memorandum will also clarify the responsibility of State and local educational agencies (SEAs and LEAs) to provide special education and related services to eligible children with ADD under Part B. Finally, this memorandum clarifies the responsibilities of LEAs to provide regular or special education and related aids and services to those children with ADD who are not eligible under Part B, but who fall within the definition of "handicapped person" under Section 504 of the Rehabilitation Act of 1973. Because of the overall educational responsibility to provide services for these children, it is important that general and special education coordinate their efforts.

II. ELIGIBILITY FOR SPECIAL EDUCATION AND RELATED SERVICES UNDER PART B

Last year during the reauthorization of the Education of the Handicapped Act (now the Individuals with Disabilities Education Act), Congress gave serious consideration to including ADD in the definition of "children with disabilities" in the statute. The Department took the position that ADD does not need to be added as a separate disability category in the statutory definition since children with ADD who require special education and related services can meet the eligibility criteria for services under Part B. This continues to be the Department's position.

No change with respect to ADD was made by Congress in the statutory definition of "children with disabilities"; however, language was included in Section 102(a) of the Education of the Handicapped Act Amendments of 1990 that required the Secretary to issue a Notice of Inquiry (NOI) soliciting public comment on special education for children with ADD under Part B. In response to the NOI (published November 29, 1990, in the *Federal Register*), the Department received over 2,000 written comments, which have been transmitted to the Congress. Our review of these written comments indicates that there is confusion in the field regarding the extent to which children with ADD may be served in a special education program conducted under Part B.

A. Description of Part B

Part B requires SEAs and LEAs to make a free appropriate public education (FAPE) available to all eligible children with disabilities and to ensure that the rights and protections of Part B are extended to those children and their parents. 20 U.S.C. 1412 (2); 34 CFR ¶¶300.121 and 300.2. Under Part B, FAPE, among other elements includes the provision of special education and related services, at no cost to parents, in conformity with an individualized education program (IEP). 34 CFR ¶300.4.

In order to be eligible under Part B, a child must be evaluated in accordance with 34 CFR ¶¶300.530-300.534 as having one or more specified physical or mental impairments, and must be found to require special education and related services by reason of one or more of these impairments.[2] 20 U. S. C. 1401(a)(1); 34 DFR ¶300.5 SEAs and LEAs must ensure that children with ADD who are determined eligible for services under Part B receive special education and related services needs arising from the ADD. A full continuum of placement alternatives, including the regular classroom, must be available for providing special education and related services required in the IEP.

B. Eligibility for Part B services under the "Other Health Impaired" category

The list of chronic or acute health problems included within the definition of "other health impaired" in the Part B regulations is not exhaustive. The term "other health impaired" includes chronic or acute impairments that result in limited alertness, which adversely affects educational performance. Thus, children with ADD should be classified as eligible for services under the "other health impaired" category in instances where the ADD is a chronic or acute health problem that results in limited alertness, which adversely affects educational performance. In other words, children with ADD, where the ADD is a chronic or acute health problem resulting in limited alertness, may be considered disabled under Part B solely on the basis of this disorder within the "other health impaired" category in situations where special education and related services are needed because of the ADD.

C. Eligibility for Part B services under Other Disability categories

Children with ADD are also eligible for services under Part B if the children satisfy the criteria applicable to other disability categories. For example, children with ADD are also eligible for services under the "specific learning disability" category of Part B if they meet the criteria stated in ¶¶300.5(b)(9) and 300.541 or under the "seriously emotionally disturbed" category of Part B if they meet the criteria stated in ¶300.5(b)(8).

III. EVALUATIONS UNDER PART B

A. Requirements

SEAs and LEAs have an affirmative obligation to evaluate a child who is suspected of having a disability to determine the child's need for special education and related services. Under Part B, SEAs and LEAs are required to have procedures for locating, identifying, and evaluating all children who have a disability or are suspected of having a disability and are in need of special education and related services. 34 CFR ¶¶300.128 and 300.220. This responsibility, known as "child find," is applicable to all children from birth through 21, regardless of the severity of their disability.

Consistent with this responsibility and the obligation to make FAPE available to all eligible children disabilities, SEAs and LEAs must ensure that evaluations of children who are suspected of needing special education and related services are conducted without undue delay. 20 U.S.C. 1412(2). Because of its responsibility resulting from the

FAPE and child-find requirements of Part B, an LEA may not refuse to evaluate the possible need for special education and related services of a child with prior medical diagnosis of ADD solely by reason of that medical diagnosis. However, a medical diagnosis of ADD alone is not sufficient to render a child eligible for services under Part B.

Under Part B, before any action is taken with respect to the initial placement of a child with a disability in a program providing special education and related services, "a full and individual evaluation of the child's educational needs must be conducted in accordance with requirement of ¶300.532." 34 CFR ¶300.531. Section 300.532(a) requires that a child's evaluation must be conducted by a multidisciplinary team, including at least one teacher or other specialist with knowledge in the area of suspected disability.

B. Disagreements Over Evaluations

Any proposal or refusal of an agency to initiate or change the identification, evaluation, or educational placement of the child, or the provision of FAPE to the child, is subject to the written prior notice requirements of 34 CFR ¶¶300.504-300.505.[3] If a parent disagrees with the LEA's refusal to evaluate a child or the LEA's evaluation and determination that a child does not have a disability for which the child is eligible for services under Part B, the parent may request a due process hearing pursuant to 34 CRF ¶¶300.504-300.513 of the Part B regulations.

IV. OBLIGATIONS UNDER SECTION 504 OF SEAS AND LEAS TO CHILDREN WITH ADD FOUND NOT TO REQUIRE SPECIAL EDUCATION AND RELATED SERVICES UNDER PART B

Even if a child with ADD is found not to be eligible for services under Part B, the requirements of Section 504 of the Rehabilitation Act of 1973 (Section 504) and its implementing regulation at 34 CFR Part 104 may be applicable. Section 504 prohibits discrimination on the basis of handicap by recipients of Federal funds. Since Section 504 is a civil rights law, rather than a funding law, its requirements are framed in different terms than those of Part B. While the Section 504 regulation was written with an eye to consistency with Part B, it is more general, and there are some differences arising from the differing natures of the two laws. For instance, the protections of Section 504 extend to some children who do not fall within the disability categories specified in Part B.

A. Definition

Section 504 requires every recipient that operates a public elementary or secondary education program to address the needs of children who are considered "handicapped persons" under Section 504 as adequately as the needs of nonhandicapped persons are met. "Handicapped person" is defined in the Section 504 regulation as any person who has a physical or mental impairment which substantially limits a major life activity (e.g., learning). 34 CFR ¶104.3(j). Thus, depending on the severity of their condition, children with ADD *may* fit within that definition.

B. Programs and Services Under Section 504

Under Section 504, an LEA must provide a free appropriate public education to each qualified handicapped child. A free appropriate public education, under Section 504, consists of regular or special education and related aids and services that are designed to meet the individual student's needs and based on adherence to the regulatory requirements on educational setting, evaluation, placement, and procedural safeguards. 34 CFR ¶¶104.33, 104.34, 104.35, and 104.36. A student may be handicapped within the meaning of Section 504, and therefore entitled to regular or special education and related aids and services under the Section 504 regulation, even though the student may not be eligible for special education and related services under Part B.

Under Section 504, if parents believe that their child is handicapped by ADD, the LEA must evaluate the child to determine whether he or she is handicapped as defined by Section 504. If an LEA determines that a child is not handicapped under Section 504, the parent has the right to contest that determination. If the child is determined to be handicapped under Section 504, the LEA must make an individualized determination of the child's educational needs for regular or special education or related aids and services. 34 CFR ¶104.35. For children determined to be handicapped under Section 504, implementation of an individualized education program developed in accordance with Part B, although not required, is one means of meeting the free appropriate public education requirements of Section 504.[4] The child's education must be provided in the regular education classroom unless it is demonstrated that education in the regular environment with the use of supplementary aids and services cannot be achieved satisfactorily. 34 CFR ¶104.34.

Should it be determined that the child with ADD is handicapped for purposes of Section 504 and needs only adjustments in the regular classroom, rather than special education, those adjustments are required by Section 504. A range of strategies is available to meet the educational needs of children with ADD. Regular classroom teachers are important in identifying the appropriate educational adaptions and interventions for many children with ADD.

SEAs and LEAs should take the necessary steps to promote coordination between special and regular education programs. Steps also should be taken to train regular education teachers and other personnel to develop their awareness about ADD and its manifestations and the adaptations that can be implemented in regular education programs to address the instructional needs of these children. Examples of adaptations in regular education programs could include:

> following a structured learning environment; repeating and simplifying instructions about in-class and homework assignments; supplementing verbal instructions with visual instructions; using behavioral management techniques; adjusting class schedules; modifying test delivery; using tape recorders, computer-aided instruction, and other audio-visual equipment; selecting modified textbooks or workbooks; and tailoring homework assignments.

Other provisions range from consultation to special resources and may include reducing class size; use of one-on-one tutorials; classroom aides and note takers; involvement of a "services coordinator" to oversee implementation of special programs and services; and possible modification of nonacademic times, such as lunchroom, recess, and physical education.

Through the use of appropriate adaptations and interventions in regular classes, many of which may be required by Section 504, the Department believes that LEAs will be able to effectively address the instructional needs of many children with ADD.

C. Procedural Safeguards Under Section 504

Procedural safeguards under the Section 504 regulation are stated more generally than in Part B. The Section 504 regulation requires the

LEA to make available a system of procedural safeguards that permits parents to challenge actions regarding the identification, evaluation, or educational placement of their handicapped child whom they believe needs special education or related services. 34 CFR ¶104.36. The Section 504 regulation requires that the system of procedural safeguards include notice and opportunity for the parents or guardian to examine relevant records, an impartial hearing with opportunity for participation by the parents or guardian and representation by counsel, and a review procedure. Compliance with procedural safeguards of Part B is one means of fulfilling the Section 504 requirement.[5] However, in an impartial due process hearing raising issues under the Section 504 regulation, the impartial hearing officer must make a determination based upon that regulation.

V. CONCLUSION

Congress and the Department have recognized the need for providing information and assistance to teachers, administrators, parents, and other interested persons regarding the identification, evaluation, and instructional needs of children with ADD. The Department has formed a work group to explore strategies across principal offices to address this issue. The work group also plans to identify some ways that the Department can work with the education associations to cooperatively consider the programs and services needed by children with ADD across special and regular education.

In fiscal year 1991, the Congress appropriated funds for the Department to synthesize and disseminate current knowledge related to ADD. Four centers will be established in Fall 1991, to analyze and synthesize the current research literature on ADD relating to identification, assessment, and interventions. Research syntheses will be prepared in formats suitable for educators, parents, and researchers. Existing clearinghouses and networks, as well as Federal, State, and local organizations, will be utilized to disseminate these research syntheses to parents, educators and administrators, and other interested persons.

In addition, the Federal Resource Center will work with SEAs and the six regional resource centers authorized under the Individuals with Disabilities Education Act to identify effective identification and assessment procedures, as well as intervention strategies being implemented across the country for children with ADD. A document describing current practice will be developed and disseminated to parents, educators and administrators, and interested persons through the regional resource centers network, as well as by parent training centers, other parent and consumer organizations, and professional organizations. Also, the Office for Civil Rights' ten regional offices stand ready to provide technical assistance to parents and educators.

It is our hope that the above information will be of assistance to your State as you plan for the needs of children with ADD who require special education and related services under Part B, as well as for the needs of the broader group of children with ADD who do not qualify for special education and related services under Part B, but for whom special education or adaptations in regular education programs are needed.

NOTES

1. While we recognize that the disorders ADD and ADHD vary, the term ADD is being used to encompass children with both disorders.

2. The Part B regulations define 11 specified disabilities. 34 CFR ¶300.5(b)(1)-(11). The Education of the Handicapped Act Amendments of 1990 amended the Individuals with Disabilities Education Act (formerly the Education of the Handicapped Act) to specify that autism and traumatic brain injury are separate disability categories. See section 602(a)(1) of the Act, to be modified at 20 U.S.C. 1401 (a)(1).

3. Section 300.505 of the Part B regulations sets out the elements that must be contained in the prior written notice to parents:

(1) A full explanation of all of the procedural safeguards available to the parents under Subpart E;

(2) A description of the action proposed or refused by the agency, an explanation of why the agency proposes or refuses to take action and a description of any options the agency considered and the reasons why those options were rejected;

(3) A description of each evaluation procedure, test, record, or report the agency uses as a basis for the proposal or refusal; and

(4) a description of any other factors which are relevant to the agency's proposal or refusal. 34 CFR¶300.505(a)(1)-(4).

4. Many LEAs use the same process for determining the needs of students under Section 504 that they use for implementing Part B.

5. Again, many LEAs and some SEAs are conserving time and resources by using the same due process procedures for resolving disputes under both laws.

RESOURCE D:
OCR FACTS:
SECTION 504 COVERAGE
OF CHILDREN WITH ADD

Question: What is ADD?

Answer: Attention deficit disorder (ADD) is a neurobiological disability. It is characterized by attention skills that are developmentally inappropriate; impulsivity; and in some cases, hyperactivity.

Question: Are all children with ADD automatically protected under Section 504?

Answer: No. Some children with ADD may have a disability within the meaning of Section 504; others may not. Children must meet the Section 504 definition of disability to be protected under the regulation. Under Section 504, a "person with disabilities" is defined as any person who has a physical or mental impairment that substantially limits a major life activity (e.g., learning). Thus, depending on the severity of their condition, children with ADD may or may not fit within that definition.

Question: Must children thought to have ADD be evaluated by school districts?

NOTE: This document is in the public domain and was distributed by Policy Enforcement and Program Service, U.S. Department of Education in February, 1994.

Answer: Yes. If parents believe that their child has a disability, whether by ADD or any other impairment, and the school district has reason to believe that the child may need special education or related services, the school district must evaluate the child. If the school district does not believe the child needs special education or related services and thus does not evaluate the child, the school district must notify the parents of their due process rights.

Question: Must school districts have a different evaluation process for Section 504 and the IDEA?

Answer: No. School districts may use the same process for evaluating the needs of students under Section 504 that they use for implementing IDEA.

Question: Can school districts have a different evaluation process for Section 504?

Answer: Yes. School districts may have a separate process for evaluating the needs of students under Section 504. However, they must follow the requirements for evaluation specified in the Section 504 regulation.

Question: Is a child with ADD, who has a disability within the meaning of Section 504 but not under the IDEA, entitled to receive special education services?

Answer: Yes. If a child with ADD is found to have a disability within the meaning of Section 504, he or she is entitled to receive any special education services the placement team decides are necessary.

Question: Can a school district refuse to provide special education services to a child with ADD because he or she does not meet the eligibility criteria under the IDEA?

Answer: No.

Question: Can a child with ADD, who is protected under Section 504, receive related aids and services in the regular educational setting?

Answer: Yes. Should it be determined that a child with ADD has a disability within the meaning of Section 504 and needs *only* adjustments in the regular classroom rather than special education, those adjustments are required by Section 504.

Question: Can parents request a due process hearing if a school district refuses to evaluate their child for ADD?

Answer: Yes. In fact, parents may request a due process hearing to challenge any actions regarding the identification, evaluation, or educational placement of their child with a disability, whom they believe needs special education or related services.

Question: Must a school district have a separate hearing procedure for Section 504 and the IDEA?

Answer: No. School districts may use the same procedures for resolving disputes under both Section 504 and the IDEA. In fact, many local school districts and some state education agencies are conserving time and resources by using the same due process procedures. However, education agencies should ensure that hearing officers are knowledgeable about the requirements of Section 504.

Question: Can school districts use separate due process procedures for Section 504?

Answer: Yes. School districts may have a separate system of procedural safeguards in place to resolve Section 504 disputes. However, these procedures must follow the requirements of the Section 504 regulation.

Question: What should parents do if the state hearing process does not include Section 504?

Answer: Under Section 504, school districts are required to provide procedural safeguards and inform parents of these procedures. Thus, school districts are responsible for providing a Section 504 hearing if the State process does not include it.

RESOURCE E:
OFFICE OF CIVIL RIGHTS
POSITION ON ADHD

[Section] 504 requires a public elementary or secondary program to provide a free appropriate public education to each qualified person with a disability in its jurisdiction. [Section] 504 does not list specific disorders and impairments that are considered to be disabilities. It supplies a definition of disability that triggers the protection of the regulation.

Under 504, "person with a disability" means any person who has a physical or mental disability that

- substantially limits one or more major life activities,
- has a record of such a disability, or
- is regarded as having such a disability.

"Major life activities" means [these]:

- Caring for one self
- Performing manual tasks
- Walking
- Seeing

NOTE: This memorandum is in the public domain and was disseminated in February 1994 by Policy, Enforcement, and Program Service, U.S. Department of Education.

- Hearing
- Speaking
- Breathing
- Learning
- Working

The question is not what the specific disability of the individual is, but does the individual have a disability that substantially limits one or more of these major life activities? Depending on the severity of their condition, children with ADD may fit within that definition.

TECHNICAL ASSISTANCE

A "qualified person with a disability" with respect to public school [includes these people]:

- A "person with a disability" of an age during which nondisabled persons are provided such services
- A person with a disability of any age during which it is mandatory under state law to provide such services to persons with disabilities
- A person with a disability to whom a state is required to provide a free appropriate public education under IDEA

If it is determined that an individual needs or is believed to need special education or related services because of a disability, the individual must be properly evaluated and placed and provided a free appropriate public education.

There has been a problem with districts denying students an evaluation for ADD because the district is not required by the IDEA to specifically address ADD, as it is not one of the 13 disabilities listed as a disability category in the IDEA. The IDEA is a funding statute; Section 504 is a civil rights statute.

If parents believe their child has a disability, whether by ADD or any other disability, and the District has reason to believe that the child needs special education or related services, the District must evaluate the child to determine whether he or she is an individual with a disability as defined by Section 504. If the District does not believe that the child needs special education or related services and refuses to evaluate the child, the District must notify the parents of their due process rights. A person has a right to a free appropriate public education even if the cost of needed services is not reimbursable by the federal or state governments.

After the proper evaluation, if ADD is identified as substantially limiting one or more major life activities, the district is obligated under the regulation to provide appropriate services to the student. A free appropriate public education, under 504, consists of regular or special education and related aids and services that are designed to meet the student's individual educational needs and that are based on adherence to the regulatory requirements. A major difference between the regulation implementing Section 504 and the IDEA is that under 504, children with disabilities need not be in special education to receive related aids and services.

SUMMARY

1. If parents believe their child has a disability, whether by ADD or any other impairment, and the District has reason to believe the child needs special education or related services, the District must evaluate the child to determine whether he or she is an individual with a disability as defined by Section 504. If the District does not believe that the child needs special education or related services and refuses to evaluate the child, the District must notify the parents of their due process rights.

2. If the child is determined to have ADD that substantially limits a major life activity, the district must provide a free appropriate public education for the child.

3. If a parent disagrees with the evaluation or placement of their child who has ADD (or both), they are afforded the same procedural safeguards as other parents of children with disabilities.

ADD is presumed to be of neurological origin. It is usually, but not always, matched with hyperactivity. The behavior and performance of students with ADD vary to a far greater extent than that of other students. Some characteristics of ADD are [these]:

- Inattention and distractibility—difficulty focusing, short attention span, easily distracted
- Impulsivity—often shifting from one activity to another

* Overarousal—overactive, restless, and easily aroused. Hyper-activity may be typical with an ADD student.

* Disorganization—may forget materials and assignments often

* Social-skills deficits—tending to be immature, lack self-awareness and sensitivity, or both

The causes of ADD, most experts agree, are a combination of biological and environmental factors, genetics, and dysfunction of the central nervous system.

Identification of ADD is achieved through [the following]:

* Interviews

    Parent interview: focused on areas of physical, emotional and
        social development
    Teacher interview: an assessment of the individual's strengths and
        weaknesses in the school environment
    Child interview: observe the behavior of the child

* Standardized behavior rating scales

    Parent rating scales
    Teacher rating scales
    Psychoeducational measures (Intelligence/psychometric tests
        and educational achievement tests).
    Medical and laboratory examinations

Because ADD is a condition with multiple facets, most experts agree that the best approach is a combination of treatment and management approaches, and a balance among the interventions to be applied.

* Medications

* Educational strategies: These approaches vary in relation to the educational needs of the ADD student. Accommodations may involve the implementation of behavioral management programs, greater teacher supervision, or the use of a teacher's aide. Some students may require a restrictive setting, such as a resource room, self-contained classroom, or a day treatment program.

* Behavioral management strategies: positive incentive programs, negative reinforcement programs, organization, responsibility, structure, and routine for the student, psychological counseling services

RESOURCE F:
BEHAVIOR OBSERVATION
INSTRUCTIONS

I. Behaviors to be Observed
   A. Choose behaviors that are observable; avoid inferences (e.g., "he hits, kicks, pokes" rather than "he is aggressive")
   B. Define the behavior to be observed
      1. "Off-task" behavior:
         a. Verbal off-task: spoken comments unrelated to assigned task
         b. Motor off-task: extraneous movements not related to assigned task (e.g., poking, tripping, throwing paper)
         c. Passive off-task: listening to or looking at something or someone not related to assigned work: daydreaming, sleeping, or sulking
      2. "On-task" behavior: quiet, working, sitting in seat, and behaving according to teacher's directions and rules; eyes on the teacher, on own task-related materials, or on pertinent teaching materials
II. Choose Situations in Which to Observe
   A. Choose a structured versus an unstructured situation
   B. Choose the child's strongest versus weakest subject

NOTE: Reprinted by permission of West Chicago Elementary District #33, West Chicago, IL.

C. Determine which group size (large group, small group, one-to-one)

III. Choose a Comparison Student

A. Ask the teacher to suggest a few "average" (not the best-behaved or worst-behaved) students in the class

B. Randomly select a comparison student

C. Systematically observe most of the children in group (time sample)

IV. Observe and Record Behavior

A. Interval recording

1. Results in measure of number of intervals (i.e., time blocks) within which the behavior was observed to occur

2. Used when behavior occurs at a moderate but steady rate

3. Procedure

a. Select size of observation interval (e.g., 10 seconds, 15 seconds)

b. Select structure of recording procedure

1) Observe and record at same time

2) Observe and record at separate times (e.g., observe for 25 seconds; record for 5 seconds)

c. When observing student, place an "x" in the block if the behavior occurs, "0" if the behavior does not occur; if detailed information about the type of off-task behavior is desired, use "v" for verbal off-task, "m" for motor off-task, "p" for passive off-task, and "t" for on-task

d. Sum up the intervals in which behavior occurred, divide that number by total number of intervals observed

e. Report results as percentage of intervals in which behavior occurred (e.g., John was observed to be on-task or off-task during 20% of the intervals observed)

4. Whole versus partial interval recording

a. Whole interval

1) Behavior observed must occur during the entire interval

2) Use when the duration of the behavior is an important factor

3) Underestimate the actual time or number of intervals in which behavior occurred

       b. Partial interval
         1) Behavior must only be observed at any time during interval
         2) Use in most situations
         3) Overestimate actual time behavior occurs during observation period

B. Time sampling recording
  1. Results in measure of the number of times behavior was observed to occur at prespecified sampling points in time (e.g., at the end of every 10-second period)
  2. Used with behaviors that occur at moderate but steady rates; do not use for behaviors that occur very briefly
  3. Procedure
    a. Select a time sample frame as short as feasible for your situation (e.g., at the end of every 15 seconds)
    b. Observe several students during the same observation session
    c. Calculate data as described in interval recording
    d. Report results (e.g., John was observed to be on-task or off-task for 50% of the times sampled)

V. Student Observation Record Forms
  A. Classroom Observation Record Protocol—use when more specific information is desired[2]
    1. Record identifying information, date and time of observation, and so on
    2. Note reason for observation
    3. Note classroom activity during observation and specific rules in effect during classroom observation (e.g., students are allowed to talk to cooperative group members in 12-inch voices)
    4. Describe observation technique
    5. Note time intervals under "Time"
    6. Note target student observations under "Pupil" (e.g., "T," "V," "M," or use "+" and "0")
    7. Note comparison-student observations under "Comp"
    8. If time sampling whole class, note observations under "Class Scan"
    9. Record additional observations under "Anecdotal Notes"
    10. Under "Grouping," specify type of grouping (refer to Grouping Codes)
    11. Under "Teacher Reaction," note any significant teacher's reaction to the student's behavior

B. Behavior Observation Form
   1. Record identifying information
   2. Record type of observation technique, including interval size
   3. Place a mark in the box next to the type of off-task behavior observed during each interval (off-task refers to passive off-task); if the student was on-task during an interval, leave that interval blank or place a vertical slash through the entire interval to indicate that no off-task behavior was observed
   4. Add up total number of off-task behaviors observed in each category (e.g., add number of marks in vocalizing and note that under "Total"): divide the total number in each category by 40 to obtain the percentage
   5. Circle the applicable week number (weekly observations might be done over a period of time to determine the effectiveness of specific interventions or the effect of changes in medication).

RESOURCE G:
STRATEGIES AND TECHNIQUES TO ENHANCE MIDDLE AND HIGH SCHOOL CLASSROOM INSTRUCTION FOR STUDENTS WITH ADHD

ENGLISH LITERATURE

1. Have student listen to taped or recorded stories while following in the text.

2. Use a small group of class members to be the readers (by parts or sections) to the rest of the class, Reader's Theater technique.

3. Pair readers for reading assignments—put a good or average reader with a poor reader. Use cooperative learning groups to enhance student's strengths.

4. Have the teacher or an excellent reader read orally to the class, and let the student follow along in the text.

NOTE: Reprinted by permission of the Michigan Department of Education from *Attention Deficit Hyperactivity Disorder: ADHD Task Force Report.* 1993. Lansing, MI.

5. Use comic books, student or simplified (versions) synopses, films, and filmstrips with classics to encourage attention to the task.

6. For severe reading problems or blind youngsters, obtain the Talking Books for the Blind.

7. If parents are cooperative, enlist a family member to read to the student with a reading problem.

8. Use tutors outside of class—volunteers from school, community, senior citizens, and so on.

9. Review lessons frequently to build the sequence for students having some difficulty following the story line.

WRITTEN LANGUAGE

The highest form of language competence is expressive writing. It is a complex process requiring the integration of memory, sequencing, organization, vocabulary, grammar, handwriting, spelling, ideation, and conceptualization. Skills in this area must be taught with careful planning, deliberate step-by-step instruction, and evaluation and feedback.

1. Encourage students to report experiences, share feelings, describe pictures, and participate in interviews and dramatic presentations.

2. Provide a variety of experiences to talk about words and develop an understanding of connotative as well as denotative meanings. Additional activities include organizing, classifying, and reordering a set of sentences to tell a story in a logical order and reporting events of a story in sequence.

3. Assist the transition from oral to written language. Experiences are reported to the teacher, who writes them in the student's own words. Once the story is written down, it is read out loud to the student. The student can then begin to understand the written language process.

4. Help the students use a "process cycle" of prewriting, drafting, editing, and sharing.

5. Consider separating the content grade from the mechanics grade. The two can be evaluated separately.

6. Consider requiring and evaluating but not grading the rough draft. Teachers can make positive comments, note errors, and make suggestions for further improvement. This encourages students to continue to strive to do their best.

7. Provide instruction in outlining. Although this is a prewriting skill, many students are unable to outline prior to writing. Outlining helps students complete a thinking process that facilitates organization.

8. Give students a partial, small assignment, and then encourage them to try a longer piece of writing.

MATHEMATICS

Many of the problems with mathematics encountered by students with ADHD stem from "math anxiety "or from lack of organization in how to attack the material. These strategies can help:

1. Assign fewer problems. If pressured from other students, assign all students varying amounts of work (alternate problems, 1-15, another group 15-30, etc., random numbered problems, etc.)

2. Have students fold paper into lines, quarters, or halves, and just work what they see until that is complete.

3. Use a tutor who prepares a sheet with wider spacing and fewer problems per page.

4. Encourage the student to use a calculator to check work. If student doesn't get the right answer, encourage him or her to ask for help on problem. Emphasis is on process because he or she knows calculator will give correct answer. This is motivating for student.

5. A student often can tell what kind of day he or she is having if we'll just ask. When giving an assignment or sheet of problems, have the student write at the top before he or she starts, how many can be done correctly. Then let the student work them, correct them, and see if he or she has met the goal. Proceed gradually to more ambitious goals.

6. For story problems, have the student read the problem and underline key words and phrases. Or have someone read story problems aloud to the student with ADHD.

7. If problems are mixed up (e.g., addition, subtraction, etc., on one page), point this out by underlining, circling, or using highlighter on the operational sign to forewarn students. Gradually phase out the use of clues.

8. Set up a system (checklist, if you will) of how to attack a math problem. Put up a chart to which students can refer.

READING AND STUDY SKILLS

1. Always introduce new words, go over their dictionary meanings, and explain how the word is related to what they will be reading.

2. Review previous vocabulary occasionally; do not expect mastery after one introduction.

3. Determine the reading level of your text. If it is too high for some of your students, assign portion of assignments, reading pairs, or something nearer students' reading level. Never expect a student to read and comprehend something very much above his or her reading level.

4. Guide student's reading with meaningful questions.

5. Teach the SQ3R method as study technique:

S—Scan or survey the section to be read.
Q—Turn all bold-face type into questions, then ask that question.
R—Read that passage; continue this until end of the section or chapter, answering the question at the end of that section.
R—Review what you have read; use the questions at the end of the passage and review the chapter by
R—Reciting them out loud and reciting the answers.

(If there are no questions at the end, make up your own from the bold type and recite the answers to those for your review.)

6. Before reading or studying, ask the student to write down everything on his or her mind and then lay it aside until after the studying is completed. This process can clear the mind for studying or reading.

REPORTS

To allow for some individual differences,

1. Let some students do oral reports—this can be done face-to-face, such as one person to others in small groups, with each student rating the speaker to a checklist (need to use caution that the checklist is fully understood).
2. Let groups discuss topics and select a reporter to give feedback to the large group.
3. Let a student tape an oral report (may or may not require a brief written outline).
4. Submit written reports; allow for variations such as illustrations with the report or a series of illustrations with captions, which can be substituted for a written report.
5. Write or prepare a report for a younger group of children and go to their class at prearranged time to give it.

SCIENCE

1. Form lab groups with a mixture of students who have varying abilities and talents. (One student may be skilled reader, where another may be good at setting up complicated lab apparatus).
2. Make science a living thing rather than an emphasis on textbook material. Take science out of the classroom.
3. See suggestions under other categories as well.

SOCIAL SCIENCES

See the literature suggestions for additional help that also apply to the social sciences.

1. Obtain a variety of books covering the various topics that are being studied and individualize poorer readers' assignments to something within their reading ability.
2. Extend the social sciences into the community. Relate history to older people in the area who have community history to tell. In

studying the World Wars or the Korean or Vietnam Wars, bring in community members who can relate their war experiences (both at home and abroad).

3. Make social sciences as realistic as possible. If studying the Old West, obtain a collection of antiques or artifacts to bring in.

TESTS AND/OR EVALUATIONS

1. Avoid true-false tests. They emphasize reading and trick reading at that.

2. If possible, change the emphasis in your teaching to learning rather than testing. If a student can do work in class but freezes on tests, find more informal ways to get an accurate assessment of the student's knowledge.

3. Teach what is important and test what is important. Trivia is not the real meaning of education, especially not for students with ADHD.

4. Try not to test too much material at one time. This tends to "overload the circuits." So, shorter, more frequent tests are better than infrequent, lengthy exams.

5. Teach and test what your objectives say you will teach and test. A straightforward, no curves approach will be much easier for students with ADHD to handle.

6. Curb any appetite for pop quizzes as a punishment to make students study. Rather, if you want quizzes, use them with warning and as a means of diagnosing how your students are learning and how you are teaching.

7. If you have presented something new or something difficult, get students' reactions of whether they understood by asking a few simple questions. Have students respond to a few basic questions on the "feeling wheel."

8. Use a pictorial test for a change.

9. Interview the student to determine what he or she knows. Grading and evaluation should be open, not a surprise. Try to test according to individual abilities.

10. Give tests orally if students need that type of assistance. This can be done with a teacher, a volunteer, or any other available adult. You can use student assistants, but select carefully and do not use a peer.

11. Tape a test and have a student use a headset in the classroom or just the tape recorder in another room. Responses can either be written or given orally with enough time allowed on tape.

GENERAL

1. When working on outlining, instead of two or three pages of a chapter, have the student outline only the two or three paragraphs that are most difficult for him or her.

2. Spelling techniques differ widely but the most common is writing the word spelled correctly for a specified number of times. In spelling, generally the student is lacking in good memory skills. The extra practice is necessary, but shorten the list of words. Then, have students really concentrate on that shorter list. Let them practice both oral and written spelling to see which way they can learn best.

3. Correct grammar is difficult to master if a student is accustomed to hearing poor grammar. Do not work on too many changes at one time. Use grammar in games for additional practice. Use spelling and grammar rules. Concentrate on a single grammar rule until it is understood. Allow for lots of practice on each rule.

4. Try making contracts with students regarding work completion. A contract implies input from both parties. A fair contract does not mean that the teacher demands something and the student delivers for some type of reward. The teacher must be willing to hear the student's side of the issue also.

RESOURCE H:
PARENTS' RIGHTS

The following is a description of the rights granted by federal law for students with handicaps. The intent of the law is to keep you fully informed concerning decisions about your child and to inform you of your rights if you disagree with any of these decisions.

You have the right to the following:

1. Have your child take part in, and receive benefits from public education programs without discrimination because of his or her handicapping condition
2. Have the school district advise you of your rights under federal law
3. Receive notice with respect to identification, evaluation, and placement of your child
4. Have your child receive a free appropriate public education. This includes the right to be educated with nonhandicapped students to the maximum extent appropriate. It also includes the right to have the school district make reasonable accommodations to allow your child an equal opportunity to participate in school and school-related activities
5. Have your child educated in facilities and receive services comparable to those provided to nonhandicapped students

NOTE: Reprinted by permission of West Chicago Elementary School District #33, West Chicago, Illinois.

6. Have your child receive special education and related services if he or she is found to be eligible under the Individuals with Disabilities Education Act (PL 101-476)

7. Have evaluation, educational, and placement decisions based on a variety of information sources and by persons who know the student, the evaluation data, and the placement options

8. Have transportation provided to and from an alternative placement setting at no greater cost to you than would be incurred if the student were placed in a program operated by the district

9. Have your child be given an equal opportunity to participate in nonacademic and extracurricular activities offered by the district

10. Examine all relevant records relating to decisions regarding your child's identification, evaluation, educational program, and placement

11. Obtain copies of educational records at a reasonable cost unless the fee would deny you access to the records

12. A response from the school district to reasonable requests for explanations and interpretations of your child's records

13. Request amendment of your child's educational records if there is reasonable cause to believe that they are inaccurate, misleading, or otherwise in violation of the privacy rights of your child. If the school district refuses this request for amendment, it shall notify you within a reasonable time and advise you of the right to a hearing

14. Request mediation or an impartial due process hearing related to decisions or actions regarding your child's identification, evaluation, educational program, or placement. You or the student may take part in the hearing and have an attorney represent you. Hearing requests must be made to:

Indicate here the individual selected by the school district to receive these requests.

15. Ask for payment of reasonable attorney fees if you are successful on your claim

16. File a local grievance

The person in this district who is responsible for assuring the district compliance with Section 504 is (name).

RESOURCE I:
HOME INTERVENTIONS

A number of interventions have been helpful for parents to implement at home so that the child can be supported at home and at
school. Though these interventions are for home use, the main focus
of these approaches is the development of techniques that address the
child's thinking about the behavior as well as the behavior itself. These
approaches fall under the technical title of Cognitive Behavior Modification. The techniques try to change problem behavior by putting
the child in control of the behavior change plan. Though parental
support may be necessary at times, the goal of all the techniques is to
develop as much independent control as possible to prepare the child
for adulthood. The interventions should be used when necessary and
are not presented in any order.

COGNATIVE BEHAVIOR MODIFICATIONS

TIME MANAGEMENT STRATEGY

Have the child draw a circle and place the things he or she has to
do around the circle in a spokelike fashion. Mark what is being
managed inside the circle. For example, if the circle is for organizing
nightly homework, the words "Tuesday's Homework" might be in the

NOTE: Reprinted by permission of the State of Virginia ADHD Task Force.

circle. Number all the items attached around the circle. Look at the amount of time available to complete the jobs. Make squares for small units of the overall amount of time. For example, 1 hour might be available for studying, so four squares would be drawn to represent 15-minute blocks of time. Have the child put the number of the item that he or she will be working on during that 15 minutes in each square so that the child is distributing the workload over the available time. Get a timer, and have the child set the timer for the first 15 minutes and begin work. The timer will help the child begin as well as stay on-task. When the timer sounds, the child asks, "How am I doing?" If the child is on schedule, the timer is reset and the child returns to work. If the child is behind schedule, he or she may increase attention or have to plan on additional time. If the child is ahead of schedule, he or she may decide to spend some time checking work or slowing down his or her speed. The strategy will help with task completion, on-task behavior, and time usage.

CHARTS

Charts are very helpful for the ADHD family. Behavior charts can make progress visual for the child and provide consequences in a systematic manner. Have the child choose one behavior that needs to be changed. The behaviors can be identified by the teacher or parent, but the child should have a choice as to what behavior to begin to change. Ask the child to draw up a chart that can be used to keep track of his or her progress. Ask the child to make a list of rewards and consequences for the chart. The chart should be as simple as possible and have spaces for each day. Plan so that the child has a chance of earning the reward. For example, don't have the reward depend on perfect behavior for an entire school day. If the child misbehaves at 9:30 in the morning, he or she has nothing to lose by misbehaving for the rest of the day. Set up the system so that the child can experience the connection between improved behavior and a reward.

SELF-REWARD

The concept of self-reward is very important for developing independence and self-control. Have the child reward himself or herself for accomplishing tasks. For example, if the child completes his or her homework, he or she will be able to choose a relaxing or fun activity.

Have the child set up the "If-Then" situation in writing and decide on the reward.

MOTIVATION

ADHD children often do not develop an awareness of the positive feelings associated with work completion because there is so much negative feeling surrounding their work. Do some work with the child, and share the positive feelings experienced. Ask the child to share his or her feelings after completing the work. As the child becomes more familiar with positive feelings, thinking about those positive feelings can be a motivational tool to help with task completion. Many ADHD children only know years of handing work in that is not satisfactory, so the feelings associated with work completion are unpleasant or numbed.

FRUSTRATION MANAGEMENT STRATEGY

ADHD children have little tolerance for frustration. They may have short fuses and blow off steam for no apparent reason or in ways that are out of proportion. Confrontation will put the child on the defensive, and imposed control will result in increased anger. The best method to handle the situation at the moment may be to diffuse the situation by recognizing the child's feelings. A statement such as

> I'm sure that you are just as angry as you can be that you studied for that test and failed anyway. That would make me want to tell somebody off or just give up. I understand how you feel, and I'd like to talk to you about it when you're ready.

The understanding may be sufficient to lessen the emotional reaction so that another intervention can take place or so that a situation does not escalate out of control.

STOP-AND-THINK APPROACHES

The old "Stop and Count to 10" philosophy can be helpful to reduce an ADHD child's impulsivity; however, rather than count to

10, a child should use a couple of questions to think about his or her action before acting. For example, asking "What will happen if I do this?" may help a child identify and think about the consequence before acting. Have the child make up his or her own question to ask before acting.

MAKING PLANS

Have the child try to develop plans whenever possible. For example, if the family has three errands to run, ask the child to make a plan to finish the errands. If a child has a lot of homework and wants to watch television, have him or her draw up a plan to manage both activities. If you are having friends over, have the child help plan the food or the activities. Everyday planning will be important modeling and practice for the ADHD child and will provide the child with a sense of accomplishment as well as participation. If the plan doesn't work, the child can try to figure out how the plan could have been changed to work better.

SOCIAL PREPARATION STRATEGY

If a holiday time or social event is upcoming and may prove to be disruptive, try to prepare the child for the event. Talk about all the things that may happen and how people should behave in the different situations. Make up possible situations or problems that may occur, and talk about possible ways that trouble could be avoided. The goal would be to help the child identify possible trouble spots as well as thinking ahead about what to do if those trouble spots occur. One of the reasons that ADHD children have difficulty in unstructured situations is that the rules for behavior are not clear. This causes the child to be anxious because his or her ability to behave appropriately may be questionable. Preparation will reduce anxiety.

DEVELOPING ALTERNATIVES

A family activity similar to charades can be helpful to enable a child to think about alternatives rather than reacting impulsively. Make up a situation or keep track of actual situations that occur at school or at home. Occasionally, choose one of the situations, and as a group, list all the possible actions that could have been taken in that situation. For example, the situation may be that the child was bumped in the lunch line and dropped his or her tray on the floor. What could happen? The following actions may be given:

- The child could say: "Did you do that on purpose?"
- The child could hit the person who bumped him or her.
- The child could knock the other child's tray on the floor.
- The child could say "I'm sorry" and help pick up the tray.
- The child could ask to talk to a teacher for help.
- The child could try to get back at the other child later.

The family members take turns acting out each different alternative. The activity is usually fun but also makes each alternative visual for the ADHD child who finds it difficult to attend to too much oral discussion. After each alternative has been acted out, the group decides on the alternative that would have worked the best and gives the reasons why.

SELF-MONITORING SYSTEMS

Any behavior that can be counted can be changed using a self-recording system. The child simply identifies the behavior to be changed and makes up a question to ask himself or herself about the behavior. For example, if the behavior is talking out in class, the question might be, "Did I talk in class today?" The child puts the question at the top of an index card and makes a mark to keep track of every time the behavior occurs. For example, a child might have three checks on an index card (or sheet of paper) under the question. That would mean that he or she talked out three times in class that day. The tracking of the behavior will help the child increase or decrease the behavior according to the desired change.

OTHER PERSON INTERVIEWS

Sometimes, ADHD children are so self-centered that they may not be aware of the impact of their behavior on others. When something bad happens or they get into trouble, they think that the other person doesn't like them or that the other person is stupid. They overlook their involvement in the situation and blame someone else. Other person interviews can be helpful to focus the child's attention on the other person's feelings. The child makes up one or two questions to ask himself or herself after he or she has done something that has resulted in trouble. For example, a child may make up the question, "How did I make the other person feel?" or "How would I have felt if I were the other person?" When a situation involving another person occurs, the question may help the child process the events so that his or her involvement is acknowledged. If the connection between the child's behavior and the resultant consequence can be made, there is a better chance for positive behavior change.

BEHAVIOR CONFERENCE

Often, the ADHD child doesn't understand the dynamics of a situation and gets carried away by the emotional components of the situation. The child may misinterpret the situation because he or she does not attend to all the details. It is important for the situation to be clarified in an unemotional manner so that the child has an understanding of the situation and the consequence he or she has received. If a child feels wronged in one situation and is allowed to continue to feel wronged, the feelings will carry over to the next situation and will make the child become more impulsive and reactive as time lapses. The child needs to look at all the pieces involved in an interaction or a situation, from an individual's viewpoint, so that an understanding is achieved. The child may still disagree with the outcome but may not continue to bear a grudge or feel wronged, which will decrease the impulsivity and the carryover to future actions.

STRESS-REDUCING STRATEGIES

The following list contains a set of more generalized home-based strategies that are recommended for parents who need help in reducing stress in their homes.

1. Structure the home environment.
2. Help your child develop good organizational skills.
3. Develop schedules and routines for your child to follow, and post them in a prominent place.
4. Have an area to which your child can go for short "time outs" when he or she needs to regain control of himself or herself.
5. Write step-by-step instructions on 3×5 index cards for each chore you expect your child to do, then have him or her refer to the card when it's time to do the next chore.
6. Have reasonable expectations that take into account the ways your child's disorder affects him or her.
7. Model tasks for your child that he or she finds difficult—repetition is often necessary to help internalize the behavior or task that is being taught.
8. Determine what rules are really important in your household, then make them very clear and concise and enforce them consistently.
9. Allow less important things to slide—pick your battles!
10. State what you want your child to do instead of what you don't want him or her to do.
11. Compile a list of rewards and consequences that are powerful motivators for your child—sit down with him or her and update the list frequently to keep it fresh and motivating.
12. Give praise and encouragement freely to motivate and reinforce good behaviors.
13. Recognize your child's effort even when he or she is not successful.
14. Show a lot of affection toward your child to reinforce that he or she is lovable.
15. Respect your child's uniqueness.
16. Try to anticipate and avoid situations that will "set off" your child.

NOTE: Reprinted by permission of the Michigan Department of Education from *Attention Deficit Hyperactivity Disorder: ADHD Task Force Report*, pp. 37-39. Lansing, MI, 1993.

17. Role play and brainstorm together with your child when problems do come up.

18. Ask for your child's perception regarding problem situations.

19. Help your child understand the part he or she plays in conflict.

20. Use a problem-solving approach, discussing with your child the advantages and disadvantages of each solution.

21. Provide your child with a daily-assignment notebook to help him or her keep track of homework assignments.

22. Provide a clutter-free study area for doing homework.

23. Strive for good communication and collaboration between home and school.

24. Set a limit for the amount of time your child can spend on homework each night, and notify school personnel that assignments may need to be modified accordingly.

25. Divide homework time into manageable work periods.

26. Involve your child in extracurricular activities he or she enjoys and at which he or she can be successful.

27. Provide opportunities that promote successful social interaction with other children (short, one-on-one, supervised play situations seem to be most successful).

28. Recognize strengths, and encourage opportunities to build them.

29. Keep emotional climate calm. Avoid "statements of judgment"; use "I-reactions" rather than "you-judgments."

30. Do not measure success by comparing your child to peers, but make him or her responsible for improvement..

RESOURCE J:
SAMPLE SCHOOL
BOARD POLICY RE:
ACCOMMODATING
INDIVIDUALS WITH DISABILITIES

In accordance with Section 504 of the Rehabilitation Act of 1973 and the Americans with Disabilities Act of 1990, discrimination on the basis of race, religion, sex, creed, handicap, pregnancy, or parenthood with respect to all educational activities and employment practices is prohibited in XYZ School District.

The administration will also convey, in the same manner, the grievance and hearing procedures established for students and employees who feel they have been discriminated against in violation of this policy. Due process rights will be afforded to students and staff who fall within the definition of Section 504 and the Americans with Disabilities Act.

The District will identify, evaluate, and provide an appropriate public education to students who are eligible for services under this policy. Reasonable accommodations shall be afforded to ensure accessibility to the educational environment and the work process.

A complete outline of procedures and activities, along with the appropriate forms, shall be kept on file by the Section 504/ADA Coordinator and are available on request.

NOTE: Reprinted by permission of West Chicago Elementary School District #33, West Chicago, IL.

The Director of Special Services is the Coordinator of Section 504/ADA activities.

Legal reference: Americans with Disabilities Act of 1990, 42U.S.C. 12111 et seq. and 12131 et seq.

28 C.F.R. Part 35.

504 RULES AND REGULATIONS

Section 1: Section 504 Requirements

A. Section 504 of the Rehabilitation Act of 1973 as amended prohibits discrimination on the basis of handicap in any program receiving federal financial assistance. As defined within section 504, a handicapped person is
   1) one who has a mental or physical disability that substantially limits one or more of that person's major life activities;
   2) one who has a record of such impairment; or
   3) one who is regarded as having such an impairment.
B. Section 504 covers a broader class of individuals who are handicapped than those covered by the Individuals with Disabilities Education Act (IDEA), formerly known as P.L. 94-142.
C. Section 504 requires that a free and appropriate education be provided students who are handicapped, regardless of the nature and severity of their handicap, and guarantees such students equal opportunity for participation in all school programs and activities.
D. For purposes of compliance with Section 504, the district (local education association [LEA]) shall
   1) screen and evaluate any student who is referred.
   2) determine the eligibility of the student based on the results of the screening and evaluation conducted by a team of knowledgeable specialists.
   3) develop a Section 504 Student Accommodation Plan for those students deemed to require services stipulating those necessary services or reasonable accommodations or both to be provided.
   4) deliver appropriate programs and services and implement reasonable accommodations in accordance with the Section 504 Student Accommodation Plan.
   5) enact procedural safeguards.

Section 2: Section 504 Definition of a Handicapped Student

A. A student who is handicapped is defined as any student who

1) has a physical or mental condition or disability that substantially limits one or more major life activities,
2) has a record of such impairment, or
3) is regarded as having an impairment.

B. "Physical or mental impairment" means

1) any physiological disorder or condition, cosmetic disfigurement, anatomical loss affecting one or more of the body systems: neurological; musculoskeletal; special sense organs; respiratory, including speech organs; cardiovascular; reproductive, digestive, genitourinary; hermic and lymphatic; skin; and endocrine or

2) any mental or psychological disorder, such as mental retardation, organic brain syndrome, emotional or mental illness, specific learning disabilities, attention deficit disorder, or attention deficit-hyperactivity disorder.

C. "Major life activity" means functions such as caring for one self, performing manual tasks, walking, seeing, hearing, speaking, breathing, and learning.

It is important to note that Congress in 1990 amended Section 504 and gave direction on drug and alcohol addiction and eligibility for Section 504 services.

1) A person who is currently using illegal drugs does not qualify under Section 504.

2) [However] General consensus is that a student who has been diagnosed as an addict, is currently using alcohol, but is not violating the School Code regarding drugs and alcohol, is eligible for services under Section 504.

3) It is generally accepted that nicotine addiction does not qualify a person for Section 504 services.

Section 3: Responsibility for Services

It is the responsibility of the district LEA to provide a free appropriate education to each qualified individual who is handicapped and who is a resident of the district, regardless of the nature or severity of the individual's handicap.

Section 4: Coordinator of 504 Activities

A. 504 Coordinator will be appointed by the district superintendent. The 504 Coordinator will be responsible for the overall implementation of this policy in each LEA.

Section 5: Evaluation Team

Once an evaluation has been conducted, a "group of persons knowledgeable about the child" must consider the results and determine if the student is eligible for services under 504. The district will determine the makeup and number of "knowledgeable persons." The LEA may use an existing group, such as the Teacher Assistance Team (TAT) or develop a new body, such as a 504 Team. The LEA will determine who will chair this team. The person who chairs the team will be fully aware of the responsibilities and the limits the Act places on the school district.

Section 6: Referral of Students With Disabilities

A. Referrals for evaluation of students for Section 504 eligibility shall be made to the school principal or designee by the parent-guardian, staff member, student, or other party.

B. The reason for referral should be documented as part of the student's temporary record, including the date the referral was received, and may include what accommodation is being requested.

C. The referral shall be directed by the school principal or designee to the TAT or 504 Team.

D. The TAT or 504 Team in each school shall be responsible for gathering and reviewing all materials and reports pertinent to the student and in the screening and evaluation of the student for Section 504 eligibility.

Section 7: Evaluation Procedures

A. A member of the TAT or 504 Team shall be responsible for explaining the procedures and obtaining a signed parent consent to complete the 504 evaluation.

B. The 504 evaluation shall be completed within a reasonable time from the date of referral.

C. Depending on the needs of the student referred, the district's evaluation will include one or more of the following: review of medical reports or other records; observation of the student, interview with the student or family or both, or evaluation with informal standardized instruments.

D. The TAT or 504 team members shall implement evaluation procedures that are

1) necessary and appropriate to determine the nature and extent of the handicapping condition or suspected handicapping condition.

2) validated for the specific purpose(s) for which they are used and are administered by trained personnel in accordance with the instructions provided by the producer.

3) tailored to assess specific areas of educational need and not merely those that are designed to measure a single general intelligence quotient.

4) selected and administered so as to best ensure that, when a test is administered to a student with impaired sensory, manual, or speaking skills, the results accurately reflect the student's aptitude or achievement level rather than the student's impaired sensory, manual, or speaking skills.

5) administered in the native language of the student or mode of communication most familiar to the person being assessed, unless it is not clearly feasible to do so.

G. To conclude that the student who has been evaluated is a student who is handicapped under Section 504, the TAT or 504 Team must confirm that

1) the student has a physical or mental condition, such as any physiological disorder or condition, cosmetic disfigurement, or anatomical loss affecting one or more of the following body systems: neurological, musculoskeletal, special sense organs, respiratory, cardiovascular, digestive, skin, and endocrine or any disorder such as mental retardation, organic brain syndrome, emotional or mental illness, or attention deficit disorder (ADD) or attention deficit-hyperactive disorder (ADHD).

2) the presence of such physical or mental impairment limits one or more of the student's major life activities, such as
a. Caring for one's self
b. Performing manual tasks
c. Walking
d. Seeing
e. Hearing
f. Speaking
g. Breathing
h. Learning

3) because of the identified handicapping condition, the student is in need of accommodations or adaptations in the regular education environment or is in need of related services.

The following examples, based on actual cases, may provide some types of "appropriate" services planned for and delivered by school districts:

Condition and Major Life Activity Affected in School	Services Provided by District
ADHD—difficulty learning (i.e., staying on task, paying attention	Reviewed existing classroom services Gave the student preferential seating Permitted the student to have shorter assignments Provided a medication administration and monitoring program
Juvenile rheumatoid arthritis— difficulty performing manual tasks, walking in school environment	Provided itinerant physical therapy and adapted PE class
Allergy to cigarette smoke— difficulty breathing in school	Administered medication during school hours Created a smoke-free environment
Student with broken leg confined to wheelchair—not able to walk in school	Reassigned some classes per a more appropriate physical location Altered the student's schedule
Drug addiction	Evaluated the student under 504 Provided support counseling at school Enrolled the student in the district truancy program
Diabetes—difficulty performing school-related manual tasks and learning	Monitored blood sugar level Provided snacks during day Prepared a written emergency medical plan
Learning problem, but *not* qualified as learning disabled under criteria—difficulty learning in school	Modified instructional content or particular classes Provided social work services Permitted alternate ways to respond to required assignments

Section 8: Eligibility Determination

A. Following the 504 evaluation within a reasonable time of the referral, the TAT or 504 Team shall meet to review the results of the evaluation.

B. The parents shall be provided written notice of the conference at least 14 calendar days prior to the conference.

C. The purpose of the conference will be for the TAT or 504 Team to determine whether the student is handicapped in accordance with Section 504 and eligible for services.

D. In deciding the student's eligibility, the TAT or 504 Team will develop recommendations concerning the services or accommodations or both needed to meet the student's educational needs.

E. The TAT or 504 Team will complete the Student Accommodation Plan documenting the nature of the concern, evaluation reports considered, evaluation results, and that the student does or does not qualify as having a physical or mental handicap that affects a major life activity under Section 504.

F. The parents of the student shall be notified in writing of the TAT or 504 Teams' decision regarding student eligibility under Section 504, including the right to an impartial due process hearing.

G. If it is determined that a student qualifies for eligibility under Section 504, the reasonable accommodation part of the Student Accommodation Plan shall be developed.

H. A review shall be conducted at least annually. A reevaluation is required before a significant change in the student's program or placement is made.

Section 9: Student Accommodation Plan

A. The Student Accommodation Plan shall be developed by the TAT or 504 Team. The plan shall list and describe the reasonable accommodations to be provided to the student based on findings and conclusions developed during the determination of eligibility.

B. The recommended reasonable accommodations may include the following:

1) Academic accommodations that involve the provision of related services, aids, consultations, monitoring services, or other methods to provide compensation for physical or mental disabilities

2) Physical accommodations that involve the provision of assistive devices for special equipment, administering medication, preferential seating, or other considerations
3) The plan shall be reviewed at least annually by the TAT or 504 Team and revised, if needed.

Section 10: Exiting from Services

If the TAT or 504 Team determines, on the basis of a review of all pertinent information, that

1) the student no longer requires any specialized services to meet the identified needs,
2) the student no longer requires any special accommodations within the regular classroom, or
3) the student can be appropriately educated in a regular classroom environment without the support, the TAT or 504 Team shall recommend termination of the student's 504 services.

Section 11: Procedural Safeguards

A. The parents shall receive a written notice of the conference to discuss the need for services, eligibility for services or accommodations or both, and the type or intensity of services or accommodations that will be provided in the regular classroom if found to be necessary. The notice will be sent 14 calendar days prior to the suggested date for the conference.
B. The parents have a right to review their child's records and have the right to representation at the conference.
C. The parents have a right to an impartial hearing and representation at this hearing.
D. The parents have a right to a review of the child's services and accommodations on a yearly basis.

Section 12: Due Process Procedures

A. In the event that parents dispute the determination of the student's eligibility for Section 504 or provisions in the Student Accommodation Plan, the parents shall document the areas of disagreement with facts supporting the conclusion.

B. The parents should contact the 504 Coordinator to establish a meeting date between the principal and parents for informally resolving the disagreement.

C. If informal resolution is unsuccessful, mediation may be used as another means for informal resolution of the disagreement.

D. If mediation is unsuccessful, the parents may request a due process hearing before an impartial hearing officer. The request for the hearing shall be in writing and specify the reasons for requesting the hearing. The request for the hearing shall be sent to the district superintendent within 5 days of the conference held to find an informal resolution to the disagreement.

E. The school district superintendent or designee shall appoint a hearing officer who is not an employee of the school district.

F. The superintendent or designee shall schedule the hearing within 15 days of the receipt of the request for the hearing.

G. During the hearing, the district representative shall present information and evidence supporting the district's position on the points of disagreement with the parents.

H. Parents may be represented by legal counsel of their choice and at their expense.

I. The parents or parent representative may present information and evidence relevant to the points of disagreement presented in the request for the hearing.

J. The hearing officer shall establish procedures for conducting the hearing and questioning school personnel and parents.

K. The hearing officer shall present a written report to the superintendent and the parents within 10 school days after the hearing. The report of the hearing shall include the issues of the case, a summary of the information presented, and a decision on the matters at issue. The hearing officer's decision shall be final.

L. If the parents wish to appeal the hearing officer's decision, they may contact the U.S. Office of Civil Rights, which enforces Section 504 of the Rehabilitation Act.

BIBLIOGRAPHY

Abramowitz, A. J. and O'Leary, S. G. (1991). Behavioral interventions for the classroom: Implications for students with ADHD. *School Psychology Review 20*, 220-234.

American Psychiatric Association. (1994). *Diagnostic and statistical manual of mental disorders*, Fourth Edition. Washington, DC: Author.

Alessi, G. Classroom observation record protocol. [Unpublished document]. Kalamazoo, MI: Western Michigan Univeristy.

Anderson, W., Chitwood, S., and Hayden, D. (1990). *Negotiating the special education maze: A guide for parents and teachers* (2nd ed.). Rockville, MD: Woodbine House.

Andrews, R., and Soder, R. (1987, March). Principal leadership and student achievement. *Educational Leadership 43*, 9-11.

Arizona Council for children with Attention Deficit Disorders. (1992). *Attention Deficit Disorder: A parent's guide*. Tucson, AZ: Author.

Armstrong, T. (1987). *In their own way: Discovering and encouraging your child's personal learning style*. Los Angeles: Jeremy P. Tarcher, Inc.

Armstrong, T. (1995). *The myth of the A.D.D. child: 50 ways to improve your child's behavior and attention span without drugs, labels, or coercion*. New York: Dutton.

Barkley, R. A. (1988). A review of stimulant drug research with hyperactive children. *Journal of Child Psychology and Psychiatry, 18*, 137-165.

Barkley, R. A. (1990) *Attention Deficit Hyperactivity Disorder: A handbook for diagnosis and treatment*. New York: The Guilford Press.

Barkley, R. A. (1994). *ADHD: What can we do?* [36-minute video, leader's guide, and manual]. Guilford Publications, Inc.

Barkley, R. A. (1994). *ADHD: What do we know?* [36- minute video, leader's guide, and manual]. Guilford Publications, Inc.

Barkley, R. A. (1994). *ADHD in the classroom* [36 minute video, leader's guide, and manual]. Guilford Publications, Inc.

Barkley, R. A. (1987). *Defiant children: A clinicians' manual for parent training.* New York: The Guilford Press.

Bateman, L., with Riche, R. (1986). *The nine most troublesome teenage problems and how to solve them.* New York: Ballantine Books.

Becker, W. C. (1971). *Parents are teachers: A child management program.* Champaign, IL: Research Press.

Braswell, L., & Bloomquist, M. (1991). *Cognitive behavioral therapy with ADHD children: Child, family, and school interventions.* New York: The Guilford Press.

Briggs, Corkvill, D. (1975). *Your child's self-esteem.* New York: Dolphin Books.

Burcham, B. G., & Carlson, L. B. (1993). Attention Deficit Disorder: School-based practices. *Executive summaries of research syntheses and promising practices on the education of children with Attention Deficit Disorder.* Washington, DC: U.S. Department of Education, Office of Special Education and Rehabilitative Services.

Camp, B. W., & Bash, M.A. S. (1981). *Think aloud: Increasing social and cognitive skills: A problem-solving program for children.* Champaign, IL: Research Press.

Cartledge, G, & and Milburn, Fellows, J. (Eds.). (1995). *Teaching social skills to children and youth,* (3rd. Ed.) New York: Allyn and Bacon.

Castellanos, X., Giedd, J. N., Marsh, W. L., Hamburger, S. D., Vaituzis, A. C., Dickstein, D. P., Sarfatti, S. E., Vauss, Y. C., Snell, J. W., Lange, N., Kaysen, D., Krain, A. I., Ritchie, G. F., Rajapakse, J. C., & Rapoport, J. L. (1996, July). Quantitative brain magnetic resonance imaging in Attention Deficit Hyperactivity Disorder. *Archives of General Psychiatry, 53,* 607-616.

Children and adults with Attention Deficit Disorder (CH. A. D. D.). (1992). *Educators Manual: Attention Deficit Disorders.* Fairfax, VA: Caset Associates.

Clabby, J. F., & Elias, M. J. (1987). *Teach your child decision making.* New York: Doubleday.

Copeland, E. D. (1990). *Attention disorders: The school's vital role* [Video]. Atlanta, GA: Resurgens Press, Inc.

Copeland, E. D. (1994). *Diverse teaching for diverse learners: A handbook for teachers and parents.* Atlanta, GA: Resurgens Press, Inc.

Copeland, E. D. (1994). *Medications for attention disorders and related medical problems.* Atlanta, GA: Resurgens Press, Inc.

Copeland, E.D., & Love, V. (1991). *Attention please: A comprehensive guide for successfully parenting children with attention disorders and hyperactivity.* Atlanta, GA: SPI Press, Inc.

Copeland, E. D., & Love, V. L. (1992). *Attention without tension: A teacher's handbook on attention disorders (ADHD and ADD).* Atlanta, GA: 3 C's of Childhood, Inc.

Dobson, J. (1974). *Hide or seek: Self-esteem for the child and his family.* Old Tappan, NJ: Fleming H. Revell Publishing Co.

Dowd, T., & Tierney, J. (1992). *Basic social skills for youth: A handbook from Boystown.* Boystown, NE: Boystown Press.

Dowd, T., & Tierney, J. (1992). *Teaching social skills to youth: A curriculum for childcare providers.* Boystown, NE: Boystown Press.

Dreikurs, R., Gould, S., & Corsini, R. J. *Family Council: The Dreikurs's technique for putting an end to war between parents and children (and between children and children).* Chicago: Henry Regnery Company.

DuPaul, G.J. (1990). *ADHD rating scale: Normative data, reliability, and validity. Unpublished manuscript.* Worcester, MA: University of Massachusetts Medical Center.

DuPaul, G. J., & Stoner, G. (1994). *ADHD in the schools: Assessment and intervention strategies.* New York: The Guilford Press.

Dykman, R. A., Ackerman, P. T., & Raney, T. J. (1993). Research synthesis on assessment and characteristics of children with attention deficit disorder. *Executive summaries of research syntheses and promising practices on the education of children with attention deficit disorder, 10-12.* Washington, DC: US Department of Education, Office of Special Education and Rehabilitative Services.

Edens, C. (1979). *If you're afraid of the dark.* New York: Green Tiger Press.

Fadely, J. L., & Hosler, V. N. (1992). *Attentional deficit disorder in children and adolescents.* Springfield, IL: Charles C Thomas Publisher.

Fine, M. J. (1977). *Principles and techniques of intervention with hyperactive children.* Springfield, IL: Charles C Thomas Publisher.

Fister, S. L., & Kemp, K. A. (1995). *Making it work on Monday.* Longmont, CO: Sopris West, Inc.

Forehand, R. L., & McMahon, R. J. (1981). *Helping the noncompliant Child: A clinician's guide to parent training.* New York: The Guilford Press.

Fowler, M. (1988). *ADD goes to school. CH.A.D.D. educators manual: Attention deficit disorders,* pp. 11-16. Fairfax, VA: Caset Associates.

Fowler, M. (1990). *Maybe you know my kid: A parent's guide to identifying, understanding, and helping your child with Attention-Deficit Hyperactivity Disorder.* Secaucus, NJ: Birch Lane Press.

Garber, S. W., Garber, Daniels, M., & Spizman, Freedman, R. (1987). *Good behavior: Over 1200 solutions to your child's problems from birth to age twelve.* New York: Villard Books.

Garber, S. W., Garber, Daniels, M., & Spizman, Freedman, M. (1990). *If your child is hyperactive, inattentive, impulsive, distractible: Helping the ADD hyperactive child.* New York: Villard Books.

Galvin, M. (1988). *Otto learns about his medicine.* New York: Magination Press.

Gittelman, M. (1981). *Strategic interventions for hyperactive children.* Armonk, NY: M. E. Sharpe, Inc.

Goldfarb, L. A., Brotherson, M. J., Summers, J. A., & Turnbull, A. P. (1986). *Meeting the challenge of disability or chronic illness: A family guide.* Baltimore: Paul H. Brookes.

Goldstein, S., & Goldstein, M. (1992). *Hyperactivity: Why won't my child pay attention.* New York: John Wiley and Sons, Inc.

Goldstein, S., & Goldstein, M. (1990). *Managing attention disorders in children: A guide for practitioners.* New York: John Wiley and Sons, Inc.

Goldstein, S., & Ingersoll, B. (1991). Controversial treatments for children with Attention Deficit Hyperactivity Disorder. In *Children and adults with Attention Deficit Disorder (CH. A. D. D.): Educators Manual: Attention Deficit Disorders,* pp. 77-78. Fairfax, VA: Caset Associates.

Gordon, M. (1991). *Jumpin' Johnny get back to work: A child's guide to ADHD/Hyperactivity.* DeWitt, NY: GSI Publications.

Gordon, M. (1992). *My brother's a world-class pain: A sibling's guide to ADHD/Hyperactivity.* DeWitt, New York: GSI Publications.

Greenberg, G. S., and Horn, W. F. (1991). *Attention Deficit Hyperactivity Disorder: Questions and answers for parents.* Champaign, IL: Research Press.

Greenhill, L. L., & Shopsin, B. (Eds.). (1984). *The psychobiology of childhood: A profile of current issues.* New York: SP Medical & Scientific Books.

Hall, R. V. (1971). *Managing behavior Part 2: Behavior modification: Basic principles.* Austin, TX: Pro-Ed.

Hall, R. V., & Hall, M. C. (1980). *How to select reinforcers.* Lawrence, KS: H & H Enterprises.

Hall, R. V., & Hall, M. C. (1980). *How to use planned ignoring.* Lawrence, KS: H & H Enterprises.

Hall, R. V., & Hall, M. C. (1980). *How to use systematic attention and approval.* Lawrence, KS: H & H Enterprises.

Hall, R. V., & Hall, M. C. (1980). *How to use time out.* Austin, TX: Pro-Ed.

Halsam, R.H., Dalby, J. T., & Rademaker, A. W. (1984). Effects of megavitamins on children with Attention Deficit Disorders. *Pediatrics, 74,* 103-111.

Hartmann, T. (1993). *Attention Deficit Disorder: A different perception.* Novato, CA: Underwood-Miller.

Ilg, F., Ames, Bates, L., & Baker, S. M. (1981). *Child behavior: Specific advice on problems of child behavior.* New York: Harper & Row.

Individuals with disabilities education Law Report 18 (19). (1992). Horsham, PA: LRP Publications.

Ingersoll, B. (1988). *Your hyperactive child: A parent's guide to coping with Attention Deficit Disorder.* New York: Doubleday.

Jacobellis v. Ohio, 378 US (1964).

Johnston, R. B. (1991). *Attention deficits, learning disabilities, and Ritalin.* San Diego, CA: Singular Publishing Group, Inc.

Jones, C. B. (1991). *Sourcebook for children with Attention Deficit Disorder: A management guide for early childhood professionals and parents.* Tucson, AZ: Communication Skill Builders.

Kelly, K., & Ramundo, P. (1993). *You mean I'm not lazy, stupid or crazy?! A Self-help book for adults with Attention Deficit Disorder.* Cincinnati, OH: Tyrell & Jerem Press.

Kendall, P., & Braswell, L. (1985). *Cognitive-behavioral therapy for impulsive children.* New York: The Guilford Press.

Kennedy, P., Terdal, L., & Fusetti, L. (1993). *The hyperactive child book.* New York: St. Martin's Press.

Kenosha Unified School District. *ADD teacher's resource guide.* Kenosha, WI: Author.

Kerr, M. M., & Nelson, C. M. (1989). *Strategies for managing behavior problems in the classroom.* New York: Macmillan.

Kirby, E. A., & Grimley, L. K. (1986). *Understanding and treating Attention Deficit Disorder.* New York: Pergamon Press.

Kohn, A. (1989, November). Suffer the restless children. *Atlantic Monthly, 90,* 264.

Koizol, L. F., Stout, C. E., & Ruben, D. H. (Eds.). *Handbook of childhood impulse disorders and ADHD: Theory and practice* (pp.148-149). Springfield, IL: Charles C Thomas.

Koplewicz, H. S. (1996). *It's nobody's fault: New hope and help for difficult children and their parents.* New York: Random House.

Krupp, J.-A., & Parker, R. (1984). *When parents face the schools.* Manchester, CT: Adult Development and Learning.

Lahey, B. (1979). *Behavior therapy with hyperactive and learning disabled children.* New York: Oxford University Press.

Lavin, P. (1989). *Parenting the overactive child: Alternatives to drug therapy.* Lanham, MD: Madison Books.

Levine, M. D. (1987). *Developmental variation and learning disorders.* Cambridge, MA: Educators Publishing Service.

Levine, M. D. (1987). *Keeping ahead in school: A student's book about learning abilities and learning disorders.* Cambridge, MA: Educators Publishing Service, Inc.

Long, N. J, & Newman, R. G. (1980). Managing surface behavior of children in school. In N. J. Long, W. C. Morse, & R. G. Newman (Eds.), *Conflict in the classroom: The education of children with problems* (4th. ed.) (pp. 233-241). Belmont, CA: Wadsworth.

Mandelkorn, T. D. (1993, May). Thoughts on the medical treatment of ADHD. *The CH.A.D.D.ER Box, 6* (3).

Mash, E. J., & Barkley, R. A. (1989). *Treatment of childhood disorders.* New York: The Guilford Press.

McEwan, E. K. (1996). *Attention Deficit Disorder.* Wheaton, IL: Harold Shaw Publishers.

McEwan, E. K. (1996). *Parents' guide to solving school problems: Kindergarten through middle school.* Wheaton, IL: Harold Shaw Publishers.

McEwan, E. K. (1996). *Seven steps to effective instructional leadership.* New York: Scholastic Press.

McEwan, E. K. (1996). The dog ate it. In E.K. McEwan, *Conquering homework hassles.* Wheaton, IL: Harold Shaw Publishers.

McInerney, M. (1994). *Effective practices for educating children with Attention Deficit Disorder.* Washington, DC: Chesapeake Institute.

McWhirter, J. J. (1977). *The learning disabled child: A school and family concern.* Champaign, IL: Research Press.

MetriTech, Inc. ACTeRS Parent Form. (1996). Champaign, IL: Author.

MetriTech, Inc. ACTeRS (ADD-H: Comprehensive teacher's rating scale. (1986, 1988, 1991). Champaign, IL: Author.

Michigan Department of Education. (1993). *Attention Deficit Hyperactivity Disorder: ADHD task force report,* p. 62. Lansing, MI: Author.

Moss, D. M. (1989). *Shelley, The hyperactive turtle.* Kensington, MD: Woodbine House.

Moss, R. A., & Dunlap, H. H. (1990). *Why Johnny can't concentrate.* New York: Bantam Books.

Novick, B. A., & Arnold, M. M. (1991). *Why is my child having trouble at school?* New York: Villard Books.

Nussbaum, N., & Bigler, E. (1990). *Identification and treatment of Attention Deficit Disorder.* Austin, TX: Pro-Ed.

Office of Civil Rights. Office of Civil Rights facts: Section 504 coverage of children with ADD. (1994, February 4). [This document was distributed by the Policy Enforcement and Program Service, US Department of Education.]

Ogan, G. D. (1994). *Can anyone help my child: Therapies and treatment for attention deficit and other learning and behavioral disorders in children, adolescents, and adults.* Abilene, TX: Faith Publishing.

O'Leary, D. K. (1984). *Mommy, I can't sit still: Coping with hyperactive and aggressive children.* Far Hills, NJ: New Horizon Press.

Osman, B. B., with Blinder, H. (1982). *No one to play with.* New York: Warner Books.

Parker, H. C. (1992). *The ADD hyperactivity handbook for schools.* Plantation, FL: Impact Publications.

Parker, H. C. (1992). *The ADD hyperactivity workbook for parents, teachers, and kids.* Plantation, FL: Impact Publications.

Patterson, G. R., & Gullion, M. E. (1976). *Living with children.* Champaign, IL: Research Press.

Phelan, T. (1993). *All about Attention Deficit Disorder.* Glen Ellyn, IL: Child Management, Inc.

Phelan, T. (1993). *All about Attention Deficit Disorder* (Video). Glen Ellyn, IL: Child Management, Inc.

Phelan, T., & Bloomberg, J. (1993). *Medication for Attention Deficit Disorder.* Glen Ellyn, IL: Child Management, Inc.

Phelan, T. (1990). *1-2-3 Magic training your preschoolers and preteens to do what you want them to do* [Video]. Carol Stream, IL: Child Management, Inc.

Phillips, D. (1989). *How to give your child a great self-image.* New York: Random House.

Quinn, P. O., & Stern, J. M. (1991). *Putting on the brakes: Young people's guide to understanding Attention Deficit Hyperactivity Disorder (ADHD).* New York: Magination Press.

Rhode, G. (1992). *The tough kid book: Practical classroom management strategies.* Longmont, CO: Sopris West, Inc.

Rhode, G. (1995). *The tough kid social skills book.* Longmont, CO: Sopris West, Inc.

Rief, S. R. (1993). *How to reach and teach ADD/ADHD children: Practical techniques, strategies, and interventions for helping children with attention problems and hyperactivity.* West Nyack, NY: The Center for Applied Research in Education.

Safer, D. J., & Allen, R. P. (1976). *Hyperactive children: Diagnosis and management.* Baltimore: University Park Press.

Schaefer, C. E., & Millman, H. L. (1981). *How to help children with common problems.* New York: Van Nostrand Reinhold, Inc. (New American Library).

Schrag, P., & Divoky, D. (1975). *The myth of the hyperactive child and other means of child control.* New York: Pantheon.

Scott, S. (1985). *Peer pressure reversal.* Amherst, MA: Human Resource Development Press.

Sheppard, W. C., Shank, S. B., & Wilson, D.. *Teaching social behavior to young children.* Champaign, IL: Research Press, 1973.

Silver, Larry B. (1991). *Attention Deficit Hyperactivity Disorder: A clinical guide to diagnosis and treatment.* Washington, DC: American Psychiatric Press, Inc.

Silver, L. B. (1993). *Dr. Larry Silver's advice to parents on Attention-Deficit Hyperactivity Disorder.* Washington, DC: American Psychiatric Press, Inc.

Silver, L. B. (1992). *The misunderstood child: A guide for parents of learning disabled children* (2nd. ed.). Blue Ridge Summit, PA: TAB Books.

Simons, R. (1987). *After the tears: Parents talk about raising a child with a disability.* New York: Harcourt Brace Jovanich.

Skaggs, J. *Behavior evaluation forms I & II.* [Unpublished undated documents].

Spizman, Freedman, R. (1985). *Lollipop grapes and clothespin critters: Quick, on-the-spot remedies for restless children 2-10.* Reading, MA: Addison-Wesley.

Stewart, M., & Olds, S. (1975). *Raising a hyperactive child.* New York: Harper & Row.

Taylor, J. F. (1994). *Helping your Hyperactive/Attention Deficit child.* Rocklin, CA: Prima Publishing and Communications.

Taylor, J. F. (1980). *The hyperactive child and the family: The complete what-to-do handbook.* New York: Everest House.

Teeter, P. A. (1991). Attention-Deficit Hyperactivity Disorder: A psychoeducational paradigm. *School Psychology Review 20,* 266-280.

Turecki, S., & Tonner, L. (1985). *The difficult child.* New York: Bantam Books.

Utah State Office of Education. The relationship of Attention Deficit Disorder to other conditions. (1994). In *The Utah Attention Deficit Disorder guide*, pp. 8-10. Salt Lake City, UT: Author.

Watson, L. S., Jr. (1973). *Child behavior modification: A manual for teachers, nurses and parents*. Elmsford, NY: Pergamon Press, Inc.

Weisberg, L. W., & Greenberg, R. (1988). *When acting out isn't acting: Conduct disorders and ADD*. Washington, DC: PIA Press.

Weiss, G., & Hechtman, Trokenberg, L. (1993). *Hyperactive children grown up*, (2nd. ed.). New York: The Guilford Press.

Weiss, L. (1992). *Attention Deficit Disorder in Adults*. Dallas, TX: Taylor Publishing.

Wender, P. H. (1987). *The hyperactive child, adolescent, and adult: Attention Deficit Disorder through the lifespan*. New York: Oxford University Press.

Whitman, B. Y., & Smith, C. (1991). Living with a hyperactive child: Principles of families, family therapy, and behavior management. In P. J. Accardo, T. A. Blondis, & B. Y. Whitman, *Attention Deficit Disorders and Hyperactivity in children* (pp. 187-211). New York: Marcel Dekker, Inc.

Wodrich, D. L. (1994). *Attention Deficit Hyperactivity Disorder: What every parent wants to know*. Baltimore: Paul H. Brookes Publishing Co.

Zametkin, A. J., Nordahl, T. E., Gross, M., King, A. C., Semple, W. E., Rumsey, J., Hamburger, S., & Cohen, A. M. (1990). Cerebral glucose metabolism in adults with hyperactivity of childhood onset. *New England Journal of Medicine 323*, 1361-1366.

Zametkin, A. J., and Borcherding, B. G. (1990). The neuropharmacology of Attention-Deficit Hyperactivity Disorder. *Annual Review of Medicine 40*, 447-451.

Zametkin, A. J., & Rapoport, J. L. (1987). Neurobiology of Attention Deficit Disorder with hyperactivity: Where have we come in 50 years? *Journal of American Academy of Child and Adolescent Psychiatry 26*, 676-686.

Zanzola, L. (1996, May). Medical experts defend against Ritalin charges. *AAP News, 10* .

INDEX

CORWIN
PRESS

The Corwin Press logo—a raven striding across an open book—represents the happy union of courage and learning. We are a professional-level publisher of books and journals for K–12 educators, and we are committed to creating and providing resources that embody these qualities. Corwin's motto is "Success for All Learners."